testimony

Pagans do not believe that man is "fallen" and do not believe there is anything from which we must be "saved." This world is not "outer darkness," but instead is the realm of flesh where we are sourced, and from which we must contact Spirit. Christianity is all about looking somewhere other than where one is, and leaving the present behind in search of an ineffable future exaltation. Pagans know the value and sacredness of the NOW, and focus on the immanent manifestations of the sacredness of this moment. We don't need a Savior, and we do need to be here now. The two are incompatible. ~ Maureen Aisling Duffy-Boose

Once we have heard the voice of our Mother, and She has embraced us, and we have found truth....no "his"-story can be sold to us again. They are "believers"....we are "knowers." ~ Summer-Jezebel Raine

Pagans have an imminent connection to our Deities every day and night. Our religion makes sense to us because it's a personal path. We don't have the insecurities they do. Have you ever had a Pagan rap on your door and say "We here to bring you the word of *insert incredibly long list of Deity names here*"? No, because most of us walk our own path and consider it the height of arrogance to try and ram it down the throat of some poor, unsuspecting Joe Average. All we can do is set a good example and maybe they will catch on and leave us alone. ~ Michael Ryan

When I became Pagan the light of Life and Love filled me and I have never looked back. I walk in Their Love and Power every day and I do not need a preacher or his book to tell me that my God/dess is real. I will never go back to being the fearful slave of a vengeful God. ~ Leo Sapphire

I cannot accept the Christian faith as it has evolved. Jesus never meant it to be what it has become! We take from many sources what feels right (for there is a grain of truth in all paths) & discard that which does not. To be slightly geeky: "The sleeper has awakened!" There is a revolution of the mind and soul taking place in the Universe and we are the center of the whirlwind. ~ Laine Wrae Thornton

The established churches have a history of political intrigue and oppression of the common people, and the Protestant churches are their self-righteous offspring – and as an elder in a Pentecostal church for 17 years, I guess I was part of their lunatic fringe! – no I can't think of one single reason to return from the open-minded, warm and fulfilling world of Paganism. ~ Richard Hatch

BOOKS BY OBERON ZELL

1. *Grimoire for the Apprentice Wizard,* with the Grey Council (New Page Books, 2004)
2. *Companion for the Apprentice Wizard*, with the Faculty of the Grey School of Wizardry (New Page Books, 2006)
3. *Creating Circles & Ceremonies: Rituals for All Seasons & Reasons*, with Morning Glory Zell (New Page, 2006)
4. *A Wizard's Bestiary,* with Ash DeKirk (New Page, 2007)
5. *Green Egg Omelette: An Anthology of Art and Articles from the Legendary Pagan Journal* (New Page, 2008)
6. *Prophecy & the End of the World (as we know it): Apocalypse or Solartopia?* with Harvey Wasserman (TheaGenesis e-book, 2012)
7. *Barsoom: A New Map of the Mars of Edgar Rice Burroughs' "John Carter of Mars" Novels* (TheaGenesis e-book, 2012)
8. *The Wizard and the Witch: An Oral History of Oberon Zell & Morning Glory*, by John Sulak with Oberon & Morning Glory Zell (Llewellyn, 2014)
9. *Death Rights & Rites* with Judith Fenley (Llewellyn Pubs, 2020)
10. *That Undiscover'd Country: A Traveler's Guide to the Afterlife* (Black Moon Pubs, 2021)
11. *Song of Gaea,* with Kirsten Johnson & Pratima Sarkar (a children's book, IngramSpark 2021)
12. *Goodbye Jesus, I've Gone Home to Mother,* with Phaedra Bonewits (Left Hand Press, 2021)

BOOKS IN PROCESS FROM OBERON...

The Wizard and the Witch: An Oral History of Oberon Zell & Morning Glory (special 2-volume expanded edition)
GaeaGenesis: Conception and Birth of the Living Earth
Creatures of Night Brought to Light
Legendary Journeys: Europe 1987, with Dona Carter
History's Mysteries
Grimoire for the Apprentice Wizard (special expanded hardcover edition)
Grimoire for the Journeyman Wizard
Walkabout of the Wandering Wizard (2018-2020)
A Wizard's Guide to Women.
Wizards of the World, with Nikki "Solaris" Kirby
Unicorns in Our Garden, with Morning Glory Zell
Handbook for My Future Parents

Goodbye Jesus, I've gone Home to Mother

Oberon Zell

with Phaedra Bonewits

Left Hand Press

Cincinnati, Ohio USA

Black Moon Manifesto
It is the Will and mission of Bate Cabal/Black Moon to effectively manifest unique and insightful occult Works for the esoteric community in a manner that is unfettered by commercial considerations.

ISBN: 1-890399-91-4
ISBN: 978-1-890399-91-7

BlackMoonPublishing.com
blackmoonpublishing@gmail.com

United States • United Kingdom • Europe • Australia • India •
Japan • Brazil

Left Hand Press
A subsidiary of Black Moon Publishing, LLC
Cincinnati, Ohio USA

dedication

I am looking out for a new perspective
Listening out for a new directive
Going back to the land of my Mother's
I will walk with my sisters and brothers
We will do what is right for each other
In our love…

~ Sebő Ferenc, "No Man's Slave"

the author

Oberon Zell earned a bachelor's degree in psychology, sociology and anthropology from Westminster College in Fulton, Missouri, and went on to graduate studies and degrees at Washington University, Harris Teacher's College, and Life Science College. His seminal work on the Gaea Thesis in the early '70s helped foster a global awareness of Earth as living Mother.

A founding father of modern Paganism (and the first to claim that label in 1967), Oberon is one of the most respected Elders in the new movement of "green religion" that emerged in the latter half of the 20th century, helping to bridge the gap between spirituality and science.

Initiated in several mystical traditions, Oberon is an ordained priest of Gaea, and co-founder of the first Pagan Church of All Worlds, incorporated in 1968. He founded the vanguard Pagan journal *Green Egg* and served as its publisher for four decades. His book titles include *Grimoire for the Apprentice Wizard, A Wizard's Bestiary,* and many others.

An international award-winning artist, Oberon has illustrated countless magazines and books since the 1960s. He is best known for his magickal jewelry and altar figurines of Gods, Goddesses, and mythical creatures. His most famous work is his revelatory sculpture of Mother Earth as "The Millennial Gaia."

Oberon is also the founder and Headmaster of the online Grey School of Wizardry, which offers more than 600 classes in 16 departments for students of all ages. After a two-year Walkabout throughout the Western Hemisphere, he is now settled in the state of Washington.

the editor

Phaedra Bonewits is an internationally-known Neopagan magician and Witch, author of *Real Energy* (New Page, 2007) which she co-wrote with her late husband Isaac Bonewits.

Phaedra has presented on the topics of magic, Tarot, and ritual at events throughout the US and Europe, has published many articles, and was a contributor to Llewellyn's 2010 Witches' Companion. She was a pioneer in public Pagan worship in Chicago, was an active public Pagan in North Carolina, and served as national vice president of the Covenant of Unitarian Universalist Pagans (CUUPS). Phaedra was also the proprietor of Explorations, the best little occult shop in downstate Illinois.

After the death of her husband, Phaedra left New York for a tourist town in southwestern Oregon where she co-leads the Coven of the Rising Phoenix.

foreword

By Chas S. Clifton

AS MARGOT ADLER FAMOUSLY WROTE IN *Drawing Down the Moon* (1989), "no one converts to Paganism or Wicca." Pagans more often speak of "coming home" or even of "de-converting," often after a period of exploring. In my own case, I left the Episcopal Church of my upbringing at about age 15, not because I was angry with anyone—I had no particularly bad experiences— but simply because Anglican Christianity did not seem to describe the cosmos or to account for everything in it. For the next five years, I was a "searcher." I read introductory books on Buddhism. I had a Bahá'í (convert) girlfriend for a time in high school and attended some local Colorado Bahá'í events. I went to lectures by Eastern teachers who were on the American scene in the Seventies, such as Swami Satchidananda (founder of Integral Yoga), Yogi Bhajan (also known as Harbhajan Singh Khalsa, founder of the 3HO movement and Sikh Dharma International) and Shunryū Suzuki, more often known as Suzuki Roshi (founder of the San Francisco Zen Center and Tassajara Monastery). All were interesting and challenging, but none spoke to my heart.

At age 21, while working a summer construction job in Taos, New Mexico, I became a Pagan, at least in my head. I did not know there were any others. Returning to my senior year of college, my "Pagan practice" was mostly writing poetry and taking long walks. For all I knew, I was the only goddess-worshipping Pagan anywhere. There was no occult bookstore where I lived, and I had not yet heard of contemporary Wiccans, Druids, and so on. Only a year later did I create my own altar and perform a self-initiation ritual (from a book that I had eventually found). Now I knew that there were Pagan groups out there. I subscribed to *Green Egg* and through its famous Forum made contact with a coven in Colorado, albeit one whose covenstead was a four-hour drive away. But now I was in the door, so speak.

So where was the "conversion"? Did it come from reading a certain book while listening to certain music, alone at night in an old adobe house? Was it standing on a headland on the Oregon coast at

Samhain of my senior year, watching the gray surf smash logs into the cliffs below and feeling the Turning of the Wheel in a way that I never had felt it before? Was it the self-initiation ritual, when I lit the candles and said the words—still wondering if the Abrahamic God would split my living room ceiling in his wrath at my apostasy? (Obviously, he did not.) Was it a powerful dream that followed some months later of being at a Wiccan sabbat, even before I had met my future high priest and high priestess?

It is not wonder that Pagans shy away from the term "conversion." It carries a lot of monotheistic baggage—the notion that if you are not with us, you must be against us. The believers versus the infidels—you must be one thing or the other. It might be better to speak of "religious mobility," a more fluid way of moving between religions. We could also speak of "disaffiliation," moving away—in this case from your birth religion—and taking on another set of attitudes. I cannot point at exactly when I was "converted." There was a definite "stabbed in the heart" initial experience, but it took a long time to work its way through my entire life to a point where I could not think of being other than Pagan—and also a point where my Paganism could embrace many things.

The concept of "conversion" often under-emphasizes the many aspects of taking on a new path. We have all encountered the "zeal of the convert," those cases where someone had adopted a new religion or new political philosophy and becomes extremely legalistic about it. All the rules most be followed, to the letter! As an aside, if you don't think that there are any rules in Paganism, you have not looked carefully enough. Just as groups claiming to work by "consensus" actually do have hierarchies but just conceal them, likewise Paganism has its rules. To give one small example: at a large Pagan gathering I was introduced to a woman whom I had never met before. Maybe because I was working in the corporate world at the time, I held out my hand, by force of habit. "Pagans *hug!*" she exclaimed, and threw herself at me.[1]

That said, it is pretty hard to be a *legalistic* Pagan, but human nature being what it is, I am sure it is not impossible. One problem rises when newcomers to Pagandom look at contemporary Pagans' lifestyles and wonder, "Do I have to do [that particular thing] to be

---

1 This was not a sexual thing. She was in fact a lesbian and in a long-term relationship.

accepted?" How do they learn what is important and what is essentially just a fashion statement? What is a "rule"—or at least a commonly accepted guideline—and what is just individual preference?

To think of "conversion" as the adoption of a given set of beliefs is to miss a lot. Granted, the monotheistic religions do tend to work that way. My Bahá'í friends had pledged that their prophet, Bahá'u'lláh (1817–1892), was the prophet of the age;[2] Muslims still regard Muhammed as the last and best prophet, whereas Bahá'u'lláh was a heretic. Several contributors to this book mention former membership in Protestant churches where music albums, posters, video games, etc. were ceremoniously burned as "forbidden" or "ungodly." It is all very black-and-white, us-and-them. But there has also been much written over the centuries on "syncretism," the process of meshing elements of two different religions. Syncretism often occurs where people have a strong emotional attachment to one set of practices but are confronted with another religion that is much more politically powerful. Their only recourse is to save elements of their old traditions while "baptizing" or otherwise making them superficially acceptable to the rulers. Such practices were seen among slaves in the African Diaspora and among European Pagans in the face of Orthodox and Catholic Christianity. It also occurred among the indigenous people of the Americas, where the stories told about other beings were re-shaped to fit—and to combat—the missionaries' stories about their god.

It also occurs on a personal level, for example, among those who call themselves "Christopagans," and refuse to stay in just one box. One Wiccan priestess—also a Methodist minister—whom I knew referred to her calling as "serving between the worlds." She admitted that Pagans often challenged her with "How can you authentically preach and teach Christianity? It is so different from Paganism, and why would you want to do it in the first place?" Her response was that Christianity has Pagan roots and that "the co-opting of Pagan festivals by Christianity has been a bonus rather than an irritant …. The wheel turns for both religions—the return of the child of light, spring renewal and resurrection, harvest home festivals,

---

2 I was told that he was also Maitreya, the Buddha-to-come foreseen by many Buddhists over the centuries. I suspect that some of his followers also believed him to be the "hidden" 12th Imam of Shiite Islam.

sacrifice and death. Allowing the insights of both paths to enrich the celebration of these holy days has been a great gift."[3]

I might note here that when I taught a class on religion in America for a Catholic college's remote-learning program, where all my students were women employed as nurses, I assigned each student to write a "religious autobiography," not unlike these chapters. It was interesting how many had at least switched Christian denominations without much thought, joining a spouse's church for the sake of the relationship. But that is not always a gender thing: I have known legalistic religious women as well as men who cared nothing about such boundaries.

"Conversion" also carries many non-theological aspects: people who "convert" change their food ways; ways of dressing; ways of approaching sex, love, and marriage; ways of relating to the other-than-human world; and more. It is interesting that food plays no great part in these accounts, yet people can be quite "religious" about food. The summer after high school graduation, I lived for a couple of months in an all-male Bahá'í commune. The leader was definitely a veteran "seeker," and at his request, we ate with chopsticks, there in northern Colorado. This had nothing at all to do with official Bahá'í doctrine, but apparently he felt that eating with chopsticks was more "mindful" or perhaps more "spiritual." So I ate my morning oatmeal with chopsticks.[4] I certainly felt set-apart, if that was the desired result. While there is no general Pagan equivalent to "kosher" or "halal," many individual Pagans do bring their tradition to bear on how to buy, grow, or hunt their food. It also would be interesting to learn how saying "Goodbye, Jesus" produced changes in other areas of people's lives.

You can go through the accounts in this book and find common elements. For example, Peter Nash was another one going on long walks and experiencing power in nature that was never even spoken about in church—that feeling that Christianity ended at the city limits was huge for me too. Oisce writes of finding the power in plants and how that blended with the feeling that "the Goddess was looking

---

3 Reverend B, "Priestess and Pastor," in Chas S. Clifton, ed., *Living between Two Worlds: Challenges of the Modern Witch* (St. Paul: Llewellyn Publications, 1996), 71.
4 I went from there to San Francisco, where familiarity with chopsticks was a plus.

for her." Yes she can also still relate to the Jesus mysteries, which is only to say that she has not "converted" or changed party membership so much but has become comfortable in polytheism. Stanley M. Nowakowski Jr. offers a similar position. Indeed most of these writers, like me, came from a background of formal religion, where they could when younger say, "We are Catholics" or whatever and where there was in fact a Jesus to say good-bye to.

For contrast, I would like some day to read personal stories from people brought up in households of "spiritual but not religious" or "nothing in particular" or even militant Marxist atheism. Households, in other words, where being "a religious person" was never experienced. How will those stories be different? To whom to what will the speakers or writers be saying good-bye? If you are raised with no particular sense of being a "religious person," would you be automatically hostile to the idea of "religion," perceiving it just as a collection of limits and "thou shalt nots?" Or would you be like someone raised on fast food who was suddenly faced with having to prepare a meal from raw ingredients? If someone in twenty years or so repeats Phaedra's and Oberon's excellent work in assembling this collection, what will it look like?

goodbye jesus, i've gone home to mother

By Oberon Zell
With Phaedra Bonewits (ed.)

contents

part III: appendix

Introduction

By Oberon Zell

"Goodbye Jesus; I've gone Home to Mother!"

T HE IDEA FOR THIS BOOK WAS CONCEIVED in a hot tub over 20 years ago, after an interfaith conference sponsored by the Covenant of Unitarian-Universalist Pagans (CUUPS), where a number of us were sharing our stories of how we found (or were found by...) the Goddess. Several were ex-Christian clergy who had left their churches and come over to Paganism and the Goddess. I thought these fascinating stories should be collected and published. I came up with this title and gathered a few submissions, but other things came up over the following years, and I just had to set the whole project aside 'til later. This is later.

I grew up in the Congregational Church. I took Confirmation, and I still remember the most important lesson: *Christian* means "Christ-like." So Christians are supposed to be like Christ. The obvious question then becomes, "what was Christ *like?*" I took that in rather deeply, and I think I have actually lived in a very "Christ-like" way, even though I eventually came to identify myself as Pagan!

I read the Bible from beginning to end—which few do. There were all these things in there that I thought were really bizarre, but fascinating. But since I'd started out reading Greek myths, it never occurred to me that this was any different, and was supposed to be the "one and only true way." And eventually I had this major epiphany—I realized that the entire Bible, from Genesis to Revelations, was the story of a specific people—the Jews. This was all about *them* as the "Chosen People" of *their* tribal God, Yahweh. Their origin mythos, their history, their commandments and rules, their kings, prophets, and prophecies, their messiah, their redemption...

But *I* wasn't Jewish! My ancestors were Celts and Teutons. The Bible was not the story of *my* people or history at all—and thus it simply was not relevant to me. Indeed, I realized that *my* people were the ones continuously mentioned throughout the Bible as "the other people" that the presumed Jewish readers were not supposed to emulate. This realization precipitated my liberation from Christianity after many years of total immersion in it. And eventually, of course, in seeking my own ethnic religious heritage, I became a Pagan. And many years later, I wrote "We are the Other People," as a definitive analysis of this whole issue. See Appendix.

My late wife Morning Glory's grandfather was a Methodist minister, and she was raised in that faith. As a teenager, she had a horse whom she loved dearly. When he died, she mentioned that he would be happy in heaven. He grandfather told her that no, animals had no souls and didn't go to heaven. That was it for her. She declared that her horse did too have a soul, and when she died she was going to the place where the horses go. If her horse wasn't good enough for the Christian heaven, then that heaven wasn't good enough for her!

Many people have dogs, cats, horses, ferrets, parrots, snakes and other companion animals and friends. No one can have such a creature in one's life and deny that it has a soul; we all know this. So I would think that those religions that claim animals have no souls should have no credibility for anything else they claim either.

From the mid-20th Century to now, there has been a marked shift in church attendance and religious affiliations. Christian churches have decried an alarming loss of membership—especially among the younger generations:

Evangelicals Fear Loss of Their Teenagers

The New York Times, October 6, 2006
By LAURIE GOODSTEIN

Evangelical Christian leaders are warning one another that their teenagers are abandoning the faith in droves.

Their alarm has been stoked by a highly suspect claim that if current trends continue, only 4 percent of teenagers will be "Bible-believing Christians" as adults. That would be a sharp decline compared with 35 percent of the current generation of baby boomers, and before that, 65 percent of the World War II generation.

Ron Luce, who founded Teen Mania, a 20-year-old youth ministry, says "...we've become post-Christian America, like post-Christian Europe. We've been working as hard as we know how to work ... but we're losing."

The board of the National Association of Evangelicals, an umbrella group representing 60 denominations and dozens of ministries, passed a resolution this year deploring "the epidemic of young people leaving the evangelical church."[5]

A 2019 report from the Pew Research Center noted that:

> The percentage of American adults who identify as Christian has continued a steady decline, dropping from 70.6% in 2007 to 65% in 2019. This has resulted in a rate of decline of 1.1 percentage points a year. If the above rate continues, then the percentage of Christians in the United States would *become a minority by the year 2033.*[6]

> Meanwhile, the religiously unaffiliated share of the population, consisting of people who describe their religious identity as atheist, agnostic or "nothing in particular," now stands at 26%, up from 17% in 2009. *Members of non-Christian religions also have grown modestly as a share of the adult population.*[7]

And now comes a new study from Arizona Christian University, conducted Feb. 2021:

> It found that only 57% of millennials identify as Christian. Compare that to 70% of Gen X and 79% of the baby boomer generation, and it's clear that millennials are a far less Christian generation than those that came before.
> Instead, millennials are turning to alternative sources to understand the universe. Some are even looking to the skies… just not the heavens.
> It's yet another sign that … Christianity's influence over young people in America is waning – in a big way.[8]

---

[5] Goodstein, Laurie, "Evangelicals Fear Loss of Their Teenagers." *The New York Times,* 10/6/2006 http://www.nytimes.com/2006/10/06/us/06evangelical.html?_r=1&th&emc=th&oref=login

[6] https://www.religioustolerance.org/decline-of-christianity-in-the-us.htm

[7] https://www.pewforum.org/2019/10/17/in-u-s-decline-of-christianity-continues-at-rapid-pace/

[8] "Goodbye Jesus: Millennials Dropping Christianity for Astrology, Magic, and Tarot." Posted Jun 1, 2021. American Worldview Inventory 2021, Cultural Research Center at Arizona Christian University; conducted Feb. 2021. N-2,000 adults 18+. www.themonastery.org/blog/goodbye-jesus-millennials-dropping-christianity-for-astrology-magic-tarot

"Wicca is one of the fastest-growing religions in the world"

Over the same period, however, there has been an "explosive growth of Witches, Wiccans and Pagans in the US,"[9] as well as in all English-speaking countries and many others across the globe. Indeed, some religion scholars have declared Neo-Paganism (including Wicca) to be "one of the fastest-growing religions in the world." [10]

This is especially true in English-speaking countries. Australian Census figures show rapid growth of Wicca and Paganism. Wiccans in Oz grew from fewer than 2,000 in 1996 to nearly 9,000 in 2001. The number of Pagans more than doubled over the same interval to 10,632. Most major Christian denominations lost followers over the same period.

> In Canada, religious data from the 2001 census showed that Wiccans and other Pagans experienced the greatest percentage growth of all religions in the country. They numbered 21,080 members in 2001, an increase of 281% between 1991 and 2001. The percentage of Canadians identifying with Christianity dropped from 90% in 1981 to 72% in 2001—about one percentage point per year. This drop is almost exactly the same in the U.S.[11]

Data on Wicca identification is sparser in the UK, the other country with a significant Wiccan population. A 2011 government census found that there were 12,000 Wiccans in England and Wales, but previous surveys didn't collect data on the group.[12]

> *[In England and Wales in 2011]* 240,000 people (0.4 per cent) identified with religions which did not fall into any of the main religious categories. The most common groups were Pagan and

---

[9] Sangeeta Singh-Kurtz & Dan Kopf, "the us witch population has seen an astronomical rise," quartz, 10/4/2018. https://qz.com/quartzy/1411909/the-explosive-growth-of-witches-wiccans-and-pagans-in-the-us/
[10] Prof. Ronald Hutton, "A very British Witchcraft" – youtube video
[11] Ontario Consultants on Religious Tolerance. Http://www.religioustolerance.org/wic_news.htm
[12] "The US Witch Population Has Seen an Astronomical Rise." Https://qz.com/quartzy/1411909/the-explosive-growth-of-witches-wiccans-and-pagans-in-the-us/

Spiritualist, accounting for 57,000 people and 39,000 people respectively.[13]

We really have no definitive census of Pagan numbers in America, as questions of religious identity were removed from the U.S. Census as of 1990. However, estimates based on publishers' records of Pagan-themed book sales (specifically *Drawing Down the Moon* and *The Spiral Dance*) suggest numbers into the millions. Probably the most reliable source of data is the American Religious Identification Survey:

> The American Religious Identification Survey gives Wicca an average annual growth of 143% for the period 1990 to 2001 (from 8,000 to 134,000 – U.S. data / similar for Canada & Australia). According to *The Statesman,* Anne Elizabeth Wynn claims "The two most recent American Religious Identification Surveys declare Wicca, one form of Paganism, as the **fastest growing spiritual identification in America**."
>
> "Wicca is the fastest-growing religion in America, set to be the third largest religion by 2012," claims Marla Alupoaicei, who co-wrote the recently released book *Generation Hex* with fellow Christian author Dillon Burroughs.
>
> "The numbers of adherents are doubling every 30 months," she says.[14]

> *[In 2011]* In the United States alone, there were more than 200,000 registered witches and as many as 8 million unregistered practitioners of "The Craft," according to multiple conservative scholars who documented a report on the rise of occult activity in a collaborative work entitled *God's Ghostbusters*.[15]

The *World Christian Encyclopedia* estimates that *six million* Americans profess to be Witches. These are a sub-group of over *ten*

---

[13] "Religion in England and Wales 2011." Https://www.ons.gov.uk/peoplepopulationandcommunity/culturalidentity/religion/articles/religioninenglandandwales2011/2012-12-11

[14] Snyder, Michael, "The Fastest Growing Religion in America is Witchcraft." http://thetruthwins.com/archives/the-fastest-growing-religion-in-america-is-witchcraft

[15] Sun, Eryn, "Vampire, Occult Entertainment Going Too Far? Christian Leaders Urge Action." Christian Post, 10/11/2011. https://www.christianpost.com/news/vampire-occult-entertainment-going-too-far-christian-leaders-urge-action

million persons the Encyclopedia says call themselves *Pagans,* who practice "primitive" religions such as "Druidism, Odin worship and Native American shamanism."[16] However, those figures from Christian sources are far higher than other estimates:

> From 1990 to 2008, Trinity College in Connecticut ran three large, detailed religion surveys. Those have shown that Wicca grew tremendously over this period. From an estimated 8,000 Wiccans in 1990, they found there were about 340,000 practitioners in 2008. They also estimated there were around 340,000 Pagans in 2008.
> Although Trinity College hasn't run a survey since 2008, the Pew Research Center picked up the baton in 2014. It found that 0.4% of Americans, or around 1 to 1.5 million people, identify as Wicca or Pagan—which suggests continued robust growth for the communities.[17]

Based on this and subsequent surveys, Religioustolerance.org provides a more current estimate. Oddly, however, they conflate all modern Pagans under the generic category of "Wicca" rather than "Paganism," as should be the case:

> We conclude that the best estimate we can make, based on inadequate hard data, is that the number of Wiccan *[i.e. Pagan]* adults in the U.S. had increased from 602,000 in 2008 to *two million* by the end of 2015. If one were to include teens, which religious surveys generally don't, we estimate over **three million** *[Pagan]* practitioners were active in the U.S. by mid-2018!
> This number is believed to be significantly lower than the actual value because many *[Pagans]* would probably be among the 5.4% of respondents who refused to reveal their religion in the 2008 ARIS study. Also … many *[Pagans]* probably do respond to a polling question but give a wrong answer.[18]

---

[16] Rufus, Sharon, "Who Are the Witches?" *Fate* (1986 Aug): quoted by Nelson Price in *"New Age, the Occult and Lion Country,"* Power Books (1989), p. 98.
[17] Sangeeta Singh-Kurtz & Dan Kopf, *Ibid.*
[18] http://www.religioustolerance.org/estimated-number-of-wiccans-in-the-united-states-7.htm

Pagan Growth in U.S. (according to ReligiousTolerance.org)

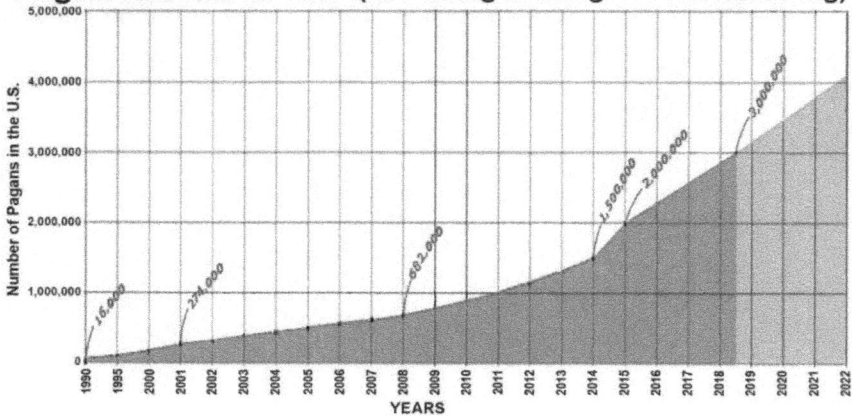

So, with *three million* adherents as of mid-2018 (projected to exceed four million by 2022…), modern Paganism (including Wicca) is now ranked as *the second-largest religion in the United States* after Christianity (214.5 million, or 65% in 2019, declining by 1.1 percentage points per year), and the fastest growing in terms of percentage! (The Pew Research Center currently lists 1.9% Jews, 0.9% Muslims, 0.7% Buddhists, and 0.7% Hindus in the US.)[19]

It should also be noted that there are 15.8% *"NOTAs"* (no particular religious affiliation) in the US. This number is increasing almost one percentage point a year. Agnostics are listed at 4.0%, and Atheists at 3.1%. Many of these people could potentially identify as "Pagan" if they were presented with the option and the term.

A Global Pagan Resurgence

There is also a growing resurgence of the Old Religion (i.e. Paganism) in many non-English-speaking countries, such as Scandinavia, the Balkans (particularly Lithuania and Latvia, which were the last countries to be converted to Christianity), the Slavic countries, Greece, Japan, India, Africa, Polynesia, Australia…

In Central and South America and the Caribbean, the Pachamama ("Mother Earth") Alliance is a powerful re-affirmation of the indigenous culture and religion. In all these countries, the Old

[19] https://www.pewforum.org/religious-landscape-study/

Religion is seen as a reclaiming of lost ancestral heritage—a restoration of cultural "roots," commonly in reaction to the brutal oppression of indigenous identity under Christianity (Roman Catholic, Orthodox, Anglican, Mormon…), Islam, Colonial imperialism, and Soviet communism.

ICELAND'S PAGANS ENJOY DRAMATIC RISE

(28 March, 2017) Iceland has seen a dramatic increase in the followers of its indigenous Pagan movement in recent years, making Odin worshippers the country's fastest-growing religion.

National Statistics Bureau figures show that followers of the Asatru Association still lag far behind the established Lutheran Church, which accounts for 237,938 or almost 70% of the population and has remained stable for decades. But the total of Icelanders who revere Odin, Thor and the Goddess Freyja has leapt 50% since 2014 to 3,583, with more than twice as many male as female faithful, Morgunbladid newspaper reports.[20]

In Russia there are 800,000 Pagans called the Rodnevers, with ritual sites all over Mother Russia. Here are a couple of paragraphs from Wikipedia on modern Slavic Paganism:

SLAVIC PAGANISM TODAY

Main article: Slavic Neopaganism

For the last few decades, Slavic Paganism has gained limited popularity among the Russian public, with many web sites and organizations dedicated to the study of Slavic mythology and some who openly call for "returning to the roots."

Most of the NeoPagan movements take place in Russia and Belarus, but they also take place in other Slavic countries like Bosnia and Herzegovina, Montenegro, Serbia, Republic of Macedonia, Bulgaria, Slovenia, Slovakia, Poland, Croatia, Czech Republic and Ukraine.[21]

There has been a similar resurgence of Classical Paganism in Greece. Leaders of the movement claimed in 2005 that there were as many as 2,000 adherents to the Hellenic tradition in Greece, with

---

[20] http://www.bbc.com/news/blogs-news-from-elsewhere-39423221
[21] Wikipedia: "Slavic Mythology." Accessed 4/30/17

an additional 100,000 who have "some sort of interest." No official estimates exist for devotees worldwide.[22]

GREEK PAGANISM LEGALLY RECOGNIZED AS 'KNOWN RELIGION' IN GREECE

Cara Schultz – April 18, 2017

ATHENS, Greece—On April 9th, the Supreme Council of Ethnic Hellenes (YSEE), a religious organization working to restore the indigenous religion of Greece, announced that after more than twenty years of struggle, the Greek state has finally recognized the Hellenic Religion as a 'Known Religion' according to paragraph 17—the only form of recognition for a religion in Greece. The mentioned paragraph includes the permission to build a temple as well as the right of public exercise of any recognized religion. Prior to this, Greek Pagans did not have religious freedoms such as the ability to buy land to create houses of worship; nor could Pagan clergy perform marriage ceremonies.[23]

We should also recognize that Paganism as the Old Religion has never been fully extinguished in large areas of the world, and remains the foundation of many indigenous cultures, as among Native Americans in North, Central and South America; much of Africa, Polynesia, Melanesia, the Caribbean, and most spectacularly, India.

Speaking of India, most modern Pagans regard Hinduism as Pagan in both the Classical and indigenous sense. Many traditional Hindus agree, as in this 1991 editorial by Sivasiva Palani, Editor of *Hinduism Today*, the largest English-language publication of modern Hindus:

Pagan. The very word conjures up uneasy feelings, and images of dancers in a moon-lit meadow or nearly-naked primitives. Yet every Hindu, all 900 million of us, is a Pagan. That's right. And if we knew the real meaning of the word, we would be proudly Pagan (though you might not have the machismo to wear the T-shirt

---

[22] Wikipedia: "Hellenism." https://en.wikipedia.org/wiki/Hellenism_(religion)#Modern_groups_and_demographics

[23] http://wildhunt.org/2017/04/greek-paganism-legally-recognized-as-known-religion-in-greece.html

that Orin Lyons, an Iroquois Indian chief and New York professor, designed proclaiming himself a "Born Again Pagan.")[24]

Where did all these Pagans come from?

The modern Pagan community can be traced to various germinal events in the mid-20th century, such as the publication of Gerald Gardner's *Witchcraft Today* in 1954, which resulted in the first generation of self-identified modern Witches. However, Witchcraft as a religion was generally unknown outside of the UK until 1964, when Gardner commissioned Ray and Rosemary Buckland to bring the Craft to the US. And Gardner's "Wiccans" never thought of themselves as "Pagans."

> Religious studies scholar Sarah Pike dates the origins of contemporary Paganism to 1967, the year that Frederick Adams incorporated Feraferia and the New Reformed [Orthodox] Order of the Golden Dawn [NROOGD] was founded. That same year, the Church of All Worlds filed for incorporation as the first Pagan "church."[25]

It was on Sept. 7, 1967 that I publicly proclaimed "Pagan" as my religious identity—and that of the Church of All Worlds, which had just "come out" after five years as a secretive underground "waterbrotherhood." Prior to that self-declaration, "Pagan" was used most commonly by Christians as a derogatory term for "primitive savages" and other nonbelievers whom missionaries were supposed to go out and convert. It was always *"those* pagans," never *"us* Pagans."

And now it is, indeed, *"us* Pagans!"—with a capital "P."

All these new Pagans had to come from somewhere. The first generation of self-identified modern Pagans did not grow up in Pagan families—as many have in more recent decades. Nearly all of us grew up in Christian or Jewish homes and found our way to

[24] "Thank Goddess for Pagans!" Palani, Sivasiva, Editor, *Hinduism Today,* Feb. 1991. https://www.hinduismtoday.com/modules/smartsection/item.php?itemid=797
[25] Halstead, John, "It's been 50 years, and what have Pagans accomplished?" *The Allergic Pagan,* 4/12/2017 https://allergicpagan.com/2017/04/12/its-been-50-years-and-what-have-pagans-accomplished/

Paganism and the Goddess later in life—after we left home and went off to college, jobs, marriages, families and lives of our own. Indeed, several of the earliest Neo-Pagan groups founded in the 1960s began on college campuses—out of study groups in world mythology, cultural anthropology, history and comparative religions:

1962   On April 7 two students at Westminster College in Fulton MO share water and found a "water-brotherhood" they call *Atl*—precursor to the Church of All Worlds (CAW).

1963   The Reformed Druids of North America (RDNA) is founded at Carleton College, in Northfield, MN.

1967   The New Reformed Orthodox Order of the Golden Dawn (NROOGD) is founded at San Francisco State University.

Coming Home

In Margot Adler's landmark survey of the rise of modern Paganism, *Drawing Down the Moon,* she describes in several places the "homecoming" experience recounted so often by the people she interviewed:

> … no one converts to Paganism or Wicca. You will find no one handing you Pagan leaflets or shouting at you on a street corner. Many people come across this book, or one of hundreds of other books, in some isolated corner of America or the world. … Upon opening its pages, they often experienced a homecoming. Perhaps they said, "I never knew there was anyone else in the world who felt what I feel or believed what I have always believed. I never knew my religion had a name."[26]

How do people become Neo-Pagans? Neo-Pagan groups are quite selective. There are few converts. In most cases, word of mouth, a discussion between friends, a lecture, a book, an article or a Web site provides the entry point. But these events merely confirm some original private experience, so that the most common feeling of those who have named themselves Pagans is something like "I finally found a group that has the religious perceptions I always

---

[26] Adler, Margot, *Drawing Down the Moon: Witches, Druids, Goddess-Worshippers, and Other Pagans in America.* Viking 1979, Beacon 1986, Penguin 1996, 2006. "Prologue."

had." A common phrase you hear is "I've come home," or, as one woman told me after a lecture, "I always knew I had a religion, I just never knew it had a name."[27]

Every July since 1981, the Association for Consciousness Exploration (ACE) has put on the Starwood Festival, a six-day Neo-Pagan, New Age, multi-cultural music extravaganza; one of the largest Pagan festivals in the world, with as many as 1,800 attendees.[28] Infamous psychonaut Timothy Leary was a guest of honor at Starwood in 1992, where he opened his keynote address at the main pavilion by proclaiming:

"Now that I know about Pagans, I realize I've always been one!" (loud cheers from everyone)[29]

Welcome Home. Come on in and make yourself comfortable…

~Oberon Zell
May 13, 2021

---

[27] Adler, "A Religion Without Converts." *Ibid.*
[28] https://www.starwoodfestival.com/
[29] From transcript of Timothy Leary's keynote address at the Starwood Festival, July, 1992.

PART I:

the pagan paradigm

Goodbye Jesus, I've gone Home to Mother

the new
pagan paradigm

JUST AS THERE IS A WIDE VARIETY OF Pagan traditions, so there is considerable variety in Pagan beliefs. The beliefs listed here are those commonly held by most modern Pagan groups, but not all:

- Pagans believe that all life—human and non-human, animate and inanimate—is an expression of the Universal/Divine mind or energy, a part of which is contained in everything.

- Pagans believe that all things are interconnected and interdependent, both ecologically and spiritually. Communication and cooperation among all elements of the material and spiritual world is possible.

- Pagans believe diversity of religious expression is a part of human nature and a positive outlet for our natural urge to connect with the universe. Pagans encourage the questioning and exploration of God-images, worship forms, rituals, celebrations, and ethics; and for the most part hold creeds and dogmas to be unnecessary for spiritual growth.

- Pagans believe that a variety of views on the nature of Deity is a part of the diversity of religious expression. Pagans may image Deity as it suits their personality, level of growth, and understanding, even to the inclusion of atheism and agnosticism. Some Pagans believe in deities as conscious, self-aware Beings which may be male or female; some view deities as numinous, archetypal, or elemental Energies. Many Pagans personify their images of Deity to make them more easily understood and explored. Most Pagans have strong personal relationships with their Deities, and strive to work in cooperation with Them daily.

- Pagans believe that all life is inherently good and oriented toward its own greatest growth, potential, and fulfillment. Evil is viewed as malicious attitudes and destructive behavior, not an existential state of being.

- Pagans believe that since the nature of creation is good, salvation is unnecessary. Many cite the Wiccan ethic: "If it harms none, do what you will." This ethic may appear simplistic, but it is quite challenging to live. Although Pagan ethics seem to bring a high degree of freedom, they also bring great responsibilities. And most Pagans believe they will be held personally responsible for their choices in some fashion, either in this life, in an after-life, or in reincarnation.

- Pagans are encouraged to explore and test every idea they encounter, and to accept an idea as their own only if validated by personal experience. Pagan religious worship focuses on the experiential and utilizes singing, dance, movement, drumming, energy work, and healing.

- Paganism is not a "revealed" religion, like Christianity, Buddhism or Islam, based on the revelations and teachings of a founding prophet. Paganism is a tribal religion, like those of the Native Americans. In a revealed religion, membership in the religious community is usually defined by believing in the teachings, or scriptures. In a tribal religion, membership is determined by one's participation in the community, and belief is more a matter of personal conviction.

Who on Earth is the Goddess?

By Morning Glory and Oberon Zell, 1977

"Well, for instance, who is this All-Mother you're always talking about?"
"Why, you are, Edward...The All-Mother. You're the All-Mother, I'm the All-Mother, that little bird singing out there, it's the All-Mother. The All-Mother is everything. The All-Mother is life..."[30]

THE PRIMAL AND SUPREME DEITY OF THE ancient world, the oldest and most universally worshipped, was the Great Mother, Mother Earth, Mother Nature. Images of Her date back to Aurignacian Cro-Magnon peoples, from 27,000 years ago, and are found all over the Eurasian continent from Spain to Siberia. For thousands of years before there were any male gods, there was The Goddess, and Her worship continued unabated clear up until its violent suppression by Iron Age patrism.

When and where worship of the Mother prevailed, women and Nature were held in esteem. The Chinese called Her Kwan Yin; the Egyptians knew Her as Isis; the Navajo call Her Changing Woman. To the Greeks She was Gaea, and to many black peoples She is Yemaja. She is Aphrodite, the Goddess of Love, and She says: *"All acts of love and pleasure are my rituals."*[31] She is also the ancient Crone Hecate, who gives us both wisdom and death.

The Goddess is diversity. She represents both darkness and Light and Her worship is the reconciliation of opposites. There can be no such thing as a "Good Goddess" or an "Evil Goddess." Death is part of the natural cycle as night follows day and we accept it with grace as Her final gift. The search for Balance is the goal of Her people, and it is achieved by the acceptance of multiple paths and truths. Dion Fortune once commented that all goddesses are

---

[30] Mack Reynolds, *Of Godlike Power,* 1966, pp. 146-147
[31] Doreen Valiente, "Charge of the Star Goddess."

manifestations of the One Great Goddess whose identity is as the universal feminine spirit of Nature. What Alchemists called *Anima Mundi:* the "Spirit of the World."

"For I am the Soul of Nature, who gives life to the Universe!"[32]

The eldest and greatest aspect of the Goddess is as Great Mother Nature, the all-encompassing energy of Universal Life. Her womb is the Quasar, the white hole through which all energy pours into creation, and Her all-devouring mouth is the Black hole itself through which all matter is consumed to be reborn once again as between Her thighs the universe is squeezed from spirit. Her energy then coalesces into Matter-Mater—the Mother of all forms. She ignites, becoming the Star Goddess: Nuit, whose galactic body arching across the night sky is our Milky way. Of Her are born star systems and planets including, of course, our very own Earth Mother, Gaea.

Because of the diversity of the Goddess, She is seen as manifesting in many different aspects. She is often called The Triple Goddess, which refers to Her link in the fertility cycle where She appears as Maiden, Mother and Crone. Some ancient cultures personified this Triplicity as the waxing, full, and waning Moon, and other three-faced Goddess aspects are familiar to us as the Fates, the Graces, the Furies, the Muses, or even as Faith, Hope and Charity. Another familiar division of Her aspects is into Mother and Daughter (Demeter and Persephone), or as Sisters/Lovers (Fauna and Flora). Such polarities are also important in Her worship. Sometimes the polarity can exist with two different aspects of the Goddess representing both poles, but more commonly it is the great gender polarity, for the Goddess is a deity of sexual loving.

She is Ishtar or Aphrodite, the eternal Lover who awaits with eager arms the mortal man brave enough to risk Her immortal favor. Many men have worshipped Her as a lover, but she may never be possessed, for She belongs only to Herself. She is Parthenos, the eternal Virgin (in the pre-patriarchal meaning "of her own household"). She represents the Strong Woman—not dominant, but

---

[32] Valiente, *Ibid.*

independent. Her lovers are not truly human but divine. She has been the Beloved of many gods, and though jealous male gods eventually suppressed Her worship, She shared the co-rulership of Heaven and Earth for thousands of years of marital bliss. She is the inescapable Yin necessary for the cosmic balance of Yang/Yin. Symbols associated with Her (the Tree of Life, the Sacred Serpent, the Labryrinth) are found in all parts of the globe, at the heart of all the Mysteries, and underlying all the later accretions of successive religions. The search for Her is the search for our deepest ancestral roots.

> *I am the star that rises from the twilight sea.*
> *I bring men dreams to rule their destiny.*
> *I am the eternal Woman; I am She!*
> *The tides of all souls belong to me—*
> *Touch of my hand confers polarity—*
> *These are the moontides, these belong to me.*[33]

Honor Thy Mother

In all the cultures where She is still worshipped, there is no confusion over Her identity -- She is Nature, and She is the Earth. She is not an atavistic abstraction, not a mystical metaphor, not a construct of consciousness. Her body is of substance as material as our own, and we tread upon Her breast and are formed of Her flesh. "Walk lightly on the bosom of the Earth Mother," says Sun Bear, and traditional Native Americans agree. Cherokee shaman Rolling Thunder emphasizes that:

> "It's very important for people to realize this: the Earth is a living organism, the body of a higher individual who has a will and wants to be well, who is at times less healthy or more healthy, physically and mentally."[34]

Frank Waters, author of *Masked Gods* and *Book of the Hopi,* makes the same point:

---

[33] Dion Fortune, "Charge of the Moon Goddess"
[34] Doug Boyd, *Rolling Thunder,* 1974, p. 51

To Indians the Earth is not inanimate. It is a living entity, the Mother of all life, our Mother Earth. All Her children, everything in Nature, is alive: the living stone, the great breathing mountains, trees and plants, as well as birds and animals and man. All are united in one harmonious whole.[35]

Renowned historian Arnold Toynbee, writing in 1972 on "The Religious Background of the present Environmental Crisis," also observed that:

For pre-monotheistic man, nature was not just a treasure-trove of "natural resources." Nature was, for him, a Goddess, "Mother Earth," and the vegetation that sprang from the Earth, the animals that roamed, like man himself, over the Earth's surface, and the minerals hiding in the Earth's bowels, all partook of Nature's divinity.[36]

Before ever land was, before ever the sea,
Or soft hair of the grass, or fair limbs of the tree,
Or flesh-coloured fruit of my branches, I was—
And thy soul was in me.[37]

The Gaea Thesis

In order to understand the nature of the Earth Mother, we must first understand our own origins. Biologically, unisexual organisms are always considered to be female, since only the female brings forth life from her own body; in the act of reproduction single cells are referred to as mothers and their offspring as daughters. Each of us began our individual life as a single fertilized cell, or zygote. In the process of its innumerable divisions and multiplications, that cell kept dividing up and redistributing the very same protoplasm, with the same DNA.

That protoplasm which now courses through all of the several trillion cells of your adult body is the very same substance which

---

[35] Frank Waters, "Lessons from the Indian Soul," *Psychology Today,* May 1973, p. 63
[36] Arnold Toynbee, "The Religious Background of the Present Environmental Crisis," *International Journal of Environmental Studies,* 1972, Vol. III
[37] Algernon Charles Swinburne, "Hertha"

once coursed through the body of that original zygote. For when a cell reproduces, the mother cell does not remain intact, but actually *becomes* the two new daughter cells. And this is why, no matter how many times a cell fissions in the process of embryological development, all the daughter cells collectively continue to comprise but one single organism.

We may imagine that, should our cells have consciousness akin to our own, they may very well fancy themselves to be independent entities living and dying in a world that to them would seem to be merely an inanimate environment, blood cells racing along our arterial rivers, but we know them to be in fact minute components of the far vaster living beings that we ourselves are.

Over half a billion years ago, at the point we call "the Cambrian Explosion," complex life on Earth was conceived, as are we all, with a single living cell containing a replicating molecule of DNA. From that point on, that original cell, the first to develop the awesome capacity for reproduction, divided and redivided and subdivided its protoplasm into the myriads of plants and animals, including ourselves, which now inhabit this third planet from the Sun.

But no matter how many times a cell fissions in the process of embryological development, all the daughter cells collectively continue to comprise but one single organism. All life on Earth comprises the body of a single vast living being—Mother Earth Herself. The Moon is Her radiant heart, and in the tides beats the pulse of Her blood. The protoplasm which coursed through the body of that first primeval ancestral cell is the very protoplasm which now courses through every cell of every living organism, plant or animal, of our planet. What we call evolution is nothing less than embryology on a planetary scale!

And as in our own bodies, Earthly life was biologically female for the first 3 billion years, before sexual reproduction, complete with males, evolved around 600 million years ago. In evolutionary theory we say "ontogeny recapitulates phylogeny" (the development of the individual repeats the development of the ancestry); ancient people anticipated such scientific ideas when they intuitively conceptualized our planetary Divinity, like that first single cell, as feminine: our Mother Earth. The soul of our planetary biosphere is She whom we call Goddess.[38]

---

[38] Tim Zell, "The Gods of Nature; The Nature of Gods," *Gnostica* #15, 1973

First life on my sources first drifted and swam.
Out of me are the forces which save it or damn.
Out of me man and woman, and wild-beast and bird.
Before God was, I am.[39]

". . . Be the terror and the dread of all the wild beasts and all the birds of heaven, of everything that crawls on the ground and all the fish of the sea: they are handed over to you." (Gen. 9:2-3)

Since the Exodus, 3,600 years ago, Western Civilization has been pursuing a course that has taken it further and further from the Mother. The three great monotheistic religions of the West—Judaism, Christianity and Islam—have from their beginning actively suppressed the worship of the Goddess, and have tortured and brutally murdered millions of Her people. Today, She is all but forgotten in the hearts of Her children, and Her body lies raped and ravished in the wake of human progress. The Goddess is the concept of feminine divinity incarnate. The denial of feminine divinity results in the oppression of all women, including Mother Nature. As Toybee says:

> The thesis of the present essay is that some of the major maladies of the present-day world--for instance the recklessly extravagant consumption of nature's irreplaceable treasures, and the pollution of those of them that man has not already devoured--can be traced back in the last analysis to a religious cause, and that this cause is the rise of monotheism.[40]

This is not to say that all non-monotheistic religions have a perfect track record for the treatment of women in those societies. Certainly, Hindu cultures revere various goddesses and yet some Hindu sects are among the more sexist and female-suppressive societies in the modern world. Nevertheless, there is abundant archeological evidence to indicate that things were not always as they are now, especially in truly ancient societies like India.

---

[39] Swinburne, *Ibid.*
[40] Toynbee, *Ibid.*

Before the Aryan Indo-European invasion around 1,627 BCE many Neolithic and Bronze Age cultures, including the Harrapan culture of the Indus Valley and the Minoan people of Crete, had societies that appeared remarkably egalitarian. These societies were universally characterized by the worship of a powerful Great Mother whom the Hindu people still call Maha Devi Ma. She was later broken into a multiplicity of minor goddesses which were demoted to the position of wives or concubines of the gods.

By the time sacred writings were codified in the Vedas, the Primal Goddess Maha Devi in India had been divided into a triplicity of goddesses characterized as Creator, Preserver and Destroyer: Saraswati, Laksmi and Kali; respectively the consorts of Brahma, Vishnu and Shiva. In Greece, a similar process led to Kore, Demeter and Persephone (or Hecate) created from the original Cretan Rhea.

Once the Great Mother had been married off She became easier to control and the way was paved for Her dowry of natural wealth to be handed over to the financial control of Her divine consorts. Whether this new mythical development was a simple mirror of the social diminishment of women's rights or whether it preceded it and was invoked as a justification is really a moot point. But the land, formerly tied to matrilineal territorial clans, passed into the hands of patriarchal kings and princes who began to treat it as their private property and to lay waste to the forests in order to build vast temples and palaces to house their harems and other slaves.

The Goddess of Nature went from being the body and soul of all that lives to a wife, mother and household servant. Many traditions have given lip service to the so-called "Female Principle," either in the form of a divided identity like the Hindu Shakti or as a semi-divine emanation. But the power of the Goddess of Nature has gradually lost its ability to inspire the necessary respect and reverence once accorded to the Source and Bearer of Life.

Where are You, then, Mother,
Whose strength was before
All other powers? Your name
Is the only freedom.[41]

---

[41] Ramprasad Sen, *Grace and Mercy in Her Wild Hair;* 18th Century Bengal

Pantheism is the view that everything in Nature is alive, and that all living is Divine. In that context, then, the simplest explanation of Divinity is as "an energy field created by all living things. It surrounds us, it penetrates us, it binds the galaxy together." (Star Wars: "The Force") Thus a pantheistic theology of Immanent Divinity ("Thou Art God/dess") contrasts sharply with the theology of Transcendent Divinity ("God is Out There") promulgated by most of "The World's Great Religions."

Unlike the God worshipped by Christians, Moslems and Jews, the Goddess is not an omnipotent, omniscient, eternal and non-physical being who created the world and exists apart from it. Though Mother Nature is Life on the universal scale, Gaea, the Earth Mother is the very body and soul of this living planet, and She lives or dies as all life on this planet lives or dies...

Mother, not maker;
Born, and not made.
Though her children forsake her,
Allured or afraid,
Praying prayers to the God of their fashion,
She stirs not for all who have prayed.

"O my children, too dutiful
Towards Gods not of me,
Was not I enough beautiful?
Was it hard to be free?
For, behold, I am with you,
am in you, and of you—
Look forth now and see!"[42]

"...and if that which you seek you find not within you,
You will never find it without.
For behold, I have been with you from the beginning;
And I am that which is attained at the end of desire."[43]

---

[42] Swinburne, *Ibid.*
[43] Valiente, *Ibid.*

pagans and jesus

I'm curious to know if you thought it was possible to be a Wiccan and yet believe that Jesus Christ is God; to be monotheistic. Your opinion means a lot to me. ~Nathan

Dear Nathan,

Since Wicca is essentially a tribal-based religion rather than be-lief-based, what is important to other Wiccans is not what you *be-lieve* regarding theological matters, but that you *participate* in your coven's ceremonies, practices, celebrations, etc. and that you have common understandings regarding symbolism, correspondences, li-turgical order, etc.

What one chooses to believe regarding theological matters (God/gods, spirits, angels, saints, demons, devas, avatars, etc.) is generally considered an individual matter. However, some Wiccan and other Pagan Traditions ("denominations") do emphasize and/or worship specific deities. Some of these are monotheistic, while oth-ers are *duotheistic* (paired) or *polytheistic* (multiple).

Examples are:

The exclusive worship of the Greco-Roman Lunar/Mother God-dess Diana among Dianic Witches;

The primary (or exclusive) worship of the Egyptian Cosmic Mother Goddess Isis among Isians;

Worship of the Celtic God & Goddess pair Cernunnos & Cerid-wen (or Aradia) among British Traditional Witches;

Worship of particular cultural pantheons, such as Greek, Celtic, Egyptian, Roman, Norse, Hindu, Sumerian, etc.

Worship of the Canaanite Goddess & God Asherah & Baal among Jewitches;

Worship of Mother Nature/Mother Earth among Gaians...

Nearly all Wiccans and Pagans would, however, agree with the statement that "there are many gods, but one Spirit." Just as there are many people(s), but one Humanity.

Christians and other monotheists tend to call that one Spirit "God;" and what Pagans call "gods," monotheists would call Angels, Saints, or even demons. So it's important in such discussions to first clarify what is meant by the term "god."

Nearly all Witches and other Pagans regard Jesus as a great Prophet, Teacher, and Wizard during his life on Earth; and many are happy to regard him as one of the immortal Gods as well, having attained apotheosis. Most Pagans regard Divinity not as a specific individual being, but as a quality—like life, sentience, consciousness, love, etc.—which may manifest more or less strongly in various forms and individuals.

These widespread Pagan concepts of pantheism and immanent divinity are reflected in the Bible in the following examples:

> Psalm 82:6: *"I said, 'You are "gods;' you are all sons of the Most High."*
> John 10:34: *Jesus answered them, "Is it not written in your Law, 'I have said you are gods'?"*

In the Church of All Worlds, we express this concept in the phrase, "Thou art God/dess," spoken to each other in the deepest affection, reverence, love and respect.

Thus Wiccans and other Pagans who embrace such theology are generally happy to accept Jesus as God. After all, why should he be left out? And as with other deities (Diana, Isis, Yahweh, Allah, Buddha...) who are worshipped exclusively by their followers (in the same way that a monogamous couple may love each other to the exclusion of all others), Wiccans and other Pagans have no problem with those who choose to worship Jesus exclusively.

The problem with monotheists is not about Wiccans and Pagans accepting the Divinity of Jesus; rather it's the monotheists' denial of Divinity to everyone *else,* and their common pattern of trying to eradicate all other viewpoints, often persecuting, torturing, and even murdering adherents of more inclusive belief systems. As I'm sure you can appreciate were the shoe on the other foot, this sort of behavior does not go over well with the victims of such persecution— which Witches and other Pagans have historically been.

I hope this helps.

Bright Blessings!

~ Oberon Zell

the ultimate conspiracy: theses & antitheses

By Oberon Zell

ACK IN THE MID-1960s, THE NASCENT Church of All Worlds existed in the form of an esoteric water-brotherhood known as *Atl*, which was founded at Westminster College in Fulton, Missouri, on April 7, 1962, when, inspired by Heinlein's sci-fi novel, *Stranger in a Strange Land*, Lance Christie and I (then Tim Zell) first shared water. Our initial Mission Statement was simply "To make the world safe for people like us."

Atl (Aztec for "water") grew to about 100 members by the time we graduated in 1965. Now scattered to our respective graduate schools, or out in the world, we began a significant discussion around whether to go public or to remain underground.

Not wanting to limit ourselves to one approach or the other, we decided to do both, and so the Church of All Worlds went public as the first self-identified Pagan church on Labor Day of 1967 (I first publicly claimed the identity of "Pagan" on Sept. 7); while the Atlan Foundation continued to operate behind the scenes, eventually morphing into the present-day Association for the Tree of Life (ATL). Lance was chosen to head up the Atlan branch, and I was chosen to lead the CAW…which we proceeded to do for the rest of our lives. (Lance died of pancreatic cancer at Samhain of 2010.) Our relationship over nearly 50 years was that of Kirk and Spock (Lance being Spock).

When we decided to go public with the Church of All Worlds, Lance and I were keenly aware of the profound responsibility we were taking on in the founding of a new religion. We had both been avid students of comparative religion, and the history of Christianity. Nearly 2,000 years before our time, a gentle rabbi of Nazareth had preached a reformist doctrine of love, compassion, inclusivity, and non-judgmentalism; railing against hypocrites and exhorting the rich to give to the poor. A thousand years later, intent on world dominion under a single Emperor/Pope, his purported followers were waging brutal crusades and holy wars (surely an oxymoron...) and burning people at the stake for heresy—all in his name.

We debated this matter at great length: what had gone wrong? And more to the point, what foundations could we lay in our lifetimes for our new religion to ensure that a thousand years from now, our descendants would not be doing the same in our name?

In our analysis, we concluded that Jesus' teachings (and those of the early Church) had several fatal flaws which eventually and inevitably led to the Spanish Inquisition (bet he didn't expect that!). These were:

1. "Monothesisism:" the idea that there is but One-True-Right-and-Only-Way (OTROW) (term coined by Isaac Bonewits):
2. Monotheism (one God): Divinity as not only singular, but solely masculine—"Our Father in Heaven;"
3. Exclusivity: the idea of "the Chosen People" as a righteous elect Divinely ordained to rule over all others;
4. Missionaryism, proselytizing, and conversion ("proselytution");
5. Uniformity: that all people must believe and behave the same;
6. Heaven and Hell as eternal reward or punishment in the Afterlife ("You'll get pie in the sky when you die by and by...");
7. Patriarchalism: disempowerment of women; clergy could only be men (Priests);
8. Unsanctioned sexual relationships—indeed, sex itself—as vile, profane, and "sinful;"
9. Body shame and modesty ("They knew they were naked, and they were ashamed.");
10. Heterosexual monogamy (one man and one woman) as the only acceptable form of love and marriage;
11. Regarding Nature as inanimate, a "creation" made by God to be exploited by Man;
12. "Original sin" as disobedience and insubordination; mandated submission to "authority" (authoritarian, not authoritative);
13. "Heresy" to be punished severely (even unto torture and death) as disbelief in the official proclaimed doctrines;
14. "The Holy Roman Empire;" "One King to rule them all;" a universal empire holding dominion over all peoples under a single ruler (Pharoah, Emperor, Caesar, Czar, Fuhrer, Chairman...);

15. And perhaps most importantly, a failure of the founding prophet to write down his teachings, leaving it to others decades later to make it all up to suit themselves—and the agenda of Empire.

And we conceived of "antidotal" antithesis memes to each of these, as follows:

1. "Infinite Diversity in Infinite Combinations" (Vulcan IDIC): different strokes for different folks;
2. Polytheism, Pantheism, and Panentheism; multiple Gods as well as Goddesses;
3. Inclusivity: "We have a place set for you at our table;" all are welcome who choose to be here and play nice;
4. No missionaries or proselytution: those who would join us must seek us out on their own;
5. Uniqueness: embracing and cherishing diversity;
6. Reincarnation as an option for those who want to return; as well as multiple Afterlife options;
7. Feminism: empowerment of women; ordination of Priestesses (only Pagan religions have Priestesses);
8. Sacred sexuality in "all acts of love and pleasure;"
9. Holy nakedness: ritual and social nudity ("skyclad");
10. Polyamory: sanctioning *all* mutually consensual loving relationships, regardless of gender or number;
11. "The Gaea Thesis," "Mother Earth," "Mother Nature," animism: Nature as sacred, alive, and sentient;
12. "Harm none" and "Be excellent to each other" as our only Commandments; otherwise, "Do what thou wilt;"
13. Question everything and everyone;
14. "The United Federation of Planets" (Star Trek); "The Rebel Alliance" (Star Wars); The Iroquois Confederacy. Networks and alliances of free and sovereign peoples.
15. And finally, writing it all down while the founders are still alive!

And thus began what we came to call "The Ultimate Conspiracy" (because by the time you know enough to grok what we are all about, it's too late—you're already one of us!).

CAW became the first fully-incorporated church in modern times to claim the identity of "Pagan;" to legally ordain women as Priestesses; to sanction and perform gay and multiple marriages; to adopt ritual and social nudity ("skyclad"); and to restore and revive the ancient Cthonic Mysteries of Beltaine, Samhain, and Eleusis in the "Wheel of the Year." We were also the first to articulate and develop the "Gaea Thesis" as our foundational theology, reconciling science and religion.

At a germinal Clergy Retreat in the summer of 1985, we decided that we had accomplished our initial Mission (to make the world safe for people like us), so we updated CAW's Mission Statement as follows:

> *"The Sacred Mission of the Church of All Worlds is to evolve a network of information, mythology and experience to awaken the Divine within and to provide a context and stimulus for reawakening Gaea and reuniting Her children through tribal community dedicated to responsible stewardship and the evolution of consciousness."*

Half a century later, and well into a new civic Millennium and Zodiacal Aeon, I am proud that these powerful memes are firmly rooted in the world-wide Pagan movement and community that has grown up like a global forest from the seeds we planted so long ago. Modern Paganism is now recognized as the 2nd-largest religion in America, and the fastest-growing! *This* is the Neo-Pagan legacy!

part II:

personal accounts

jesus freaks, δruiδ chiefs, anδ the womb of mother earth

By Mark Townsend

THE SWORD EXCALIBUR'S SHARP END DUG into my shoulder blade and jagged stones pierced my knees. The discomfort was intense—I'd been warned that such rituals were demanding! My heart pounded as I awaited instructions. As I knelt in the dark, wet cave I felt like I'd been plugged into an electric socket, such was the energy of the place.

All was silent, save for the occasional droplets of water that fell from above splashing into the pool below. I raised my head and caught a few drops in my mouth. I wasn't thirsty; I just wanted to *taste* the enchantment of the moment. I wanted to suck the magic marrow out of the very 'bones' of Gaia.

'You've entered the womb of the Earth Mother,' the Druid Chief whispered, 'now prepare to be re-born into a magical new universe.' He gave a few more instructions and then left me.

I stayed for some time, knees sore and back aching, but it didn't matter; the experience was worth the pain. The Druids had prepared the place earlier, while I'd sat in solitude a little way down the hill. As I absorbed the breath-taking beauty of the Welsh mountain valley, so they transformed the cave into an exquisite grotto with candles, symbolic objects and incense.

There I knelt, gazing at an animal skull, left as a symbol of the death of my old life, illuminated by orange flickering light. Were it not for the physical discomfort I think I could have stayed there forever. I felt safe, held, loved and at one with the heartbeat of the universe. But now I had to make my way out. As I approached the light, the Druid Priestess greeted me and gave me symbolic gifts of the rite of passage. Her words were comforting, and she seemed to personify the Goddess herself.

It was an awesome experience—my initiation into the Bardic Grade of the Druid Order, and the more I think about it, the deeper

the parallels become between *it* and other ceremonies of my past—
of my *Christian* past.

Almost a decade earlier, while still working as a Priest of the
Church of England, I had undergone a magical and at times gruelling
Vision Quest in the New Mexican Desert. It was a male rite of passage, modelled on the tribal initiation rites of the world's various
native cultures. It was Catholic yet Pagan and, as with my Bardic
Initiation it, was also a ritual of death and re-birth. Lasting for five
long days and forcing me to dig deep into the hidden resources of
my own soul, the process challenged body, mind and spirit. Only
recently, during the period I spent researching for a Christo-Druidic
book, it became clear to me how this New Mexican trial was a piv-
otal event in my life—like a detonator which when triggered released a fuse that could not be stopped. It was only a matter of time
before there would be an explosion!

The fuse wire finally reacted the gelignite during the prepara-
tions for my wedding to my wife Jodie. It was early summer, 2007.
A deep inner compulsion (some call it total recklessness) caused me
to put into a motion a series of events that were to result in the loss
of my job, income, home, pension and (very nearly) wife. When we
returned from our honeymoon the demand for my resignation
awaited us.

For the previous ten years I'd had served as a Priest who had a
permanent love-hate relationship with the church.

My spiritual journey had begun back in my late teens after my
stepbrother took me to an eccentric little Pentecostal church not far
from my parents' home. It was all quite magical, and had an una-
shamedly supernatural side. 'Divine healing' and 'speaking in
tongues' were common occurrences (whatever those things actually
were).

I'd always been interested in magic and the unknown. I was also
a student of conjuring after catching the magic bug from my uncle
who taught me how to vanish a playing card by sleight of hand. My
passion for both kinds of magic survives to this day. So I joined the
church.

I gave my newfound Pentecostalism 100%, borrowing books
from the library, joining the small fellowship groups and asking a
constant flow of questions. I became an expert in weeks and, after
only a few months, had modified my dress and purged myself of any
possessions that seemed to conflict with Pentecostalism. Of course,

no one told me to dress so formally or avoid pubs and clubs. No one told me to stop smoking or drinking. No one told me to burn my martial arts costumes and awards, my rock LPs or my supernatural books and magazines. No one told me I should start giving 10% of everything I earned to the Church, but I did all those things. I was turning into what some of my work colleagues called 'a Jesus Freak!' I was starting to believe things about God, myself and other people that were completely out of character.

My sense of vocation to the ministry came very soon after my conversion but (thankfully) the very sensible Pastor was wise enough to demand some patience. He suggested I get involved in church life and offer myself for various quasi-ministerial jobs around the place. During this period I was eventually even allowed to stand at the pulpit and deliver a sermon. I remember it as if it was yesterday. There I stood, an eighteen-year-old rooky, preaching to the whole congregation for 45 minutes on the theme of Adam and Eve's fig leaves! And, yes, to me (and all those Pentecostals) they were real literal fig leaves and Adam and Eve were real literal people (oh how things have changed).

However, the Pentecostal phase didn't last for more than a few years. Eventually my naturally questioning mind broke through and I soon started to suffer from huge doubts. Things just didn't add up and no one was able to answer my questions except by throwing irrelevant Bible verses at me. It was as if these folk thought 'The Bible' or 'Jesus' were the answer to everything.

(Which reminds me of a joke: *A Sunday school teacher tried a new approach. She said, 'Today I have a question for you. What's small, grey, eats acorns and has a long bushy tail?' There was no response, so she repeated the question. Then, after a somewhat uncomfortable pause, an awkward-looking boy at the back put up his hand and said, 'Well I know the answer must be Jesus, but it sounds like a squirrel to me.'*)

One thing led to another and I ended up leaving the Pentecostal Church. But where could I go? The trouble was, I still had my sense of vocation. I needed to find a faith community where I could express my open and questioning spirituality as well as explore the possibility of ordained ministry.

Then I had a thought… *be a vicar!* The Anglican Church (UK equivalent of the Episcopal Church) was not something I was wildly attracted to but, having attended two C of E schools, I knew enough about it to suspect it might be just the place for me.

I ended up joining a local Church, doing five years training and—POW—was let loose on the extremely exciting and spiritually invigorating Church of England. Did you just detect a tongue in my cheek? Your senses were right. Sadly, the dear old C of E is currently on a crash course in self-destruction. It has become stale and dull, Rather than trying to recover some of the long-lost mystery and magic, it feels that a 'back to basics' conservatism is the way ahead. It's a sinking ship and no one seems to know what to do. It's also a very frightened institution and is being torn apart by in-fighting and arguing over stuff that the rest of the world seems to have come to terms with at least a few decades ago (e.g. women in ministry, homosexuality and interfaith matters).

I was ordained in 1996 and spend my first two years as a curate of a pretty market town. Because I was also known to be a magician (conjurer) I received many invitations to perform, ending up being nicknamed 'The Conjuring Curate.' I had a fair few TV appearances during this period.

Then I moved to my second post of Team Vicar which meant having responsibility for the largest church in the county (after the cathedral itself). It was a beautiful mediaeval priory in a quaint market town near the Welsh border. I remained in that post for eight years and though I will never regret the time, it ended up as the most disenchanting period of my life. Do not misunderstand me, I loved serving the church and town and had the privilege of getting to know hundreds of angels both inside and outside the congregation. But there were underlying pressures against which I had little or no defence, some of them un-asked for and others of my own stupid making.

I ended up hating all the Church stuff. It was just so disconnected form real life. But I loved the people-stuff, particularly when it was out there in the community. I saw my most important function as being a pastor who was there to offer service and support to the 12,000 members of the local community—to bless their babies, join together their couples and bury their departed..

There were other problems in my life, not least deep unhappiness at home. Within a few years I'd become engulfed in a black cloud of depression. It had attacked me before, but never to this extent. I sought medical help and was signed off work, put on antidepressants and allocated a counselor. It's hard enough for someone in a regular job to admit to a so-called breakdown, but for a clergyman—talk about humbling! The only thing worse was when I had to tell my congregation that my wife and I were going to divorce, which came a year or so after the breakdown. There's no need to go into the whys and ifs of that saga. It's enough to say that, like any separation (especially where children are involved) it was a painful and shattering experience.

My eventual departure from the world of official ministry had become inevitable; but it was not until June 2007 that I finally resigned. The way it all happened was quiet amazing (and very painful in the end) but it's far too long a story to tell here. For those interested please see chapter six of *The Path of the Blue Raven* (O Books 2009).

Then some six months later—quite out of the blue—something happened that dramatically changed my life. I'd been earning a living working as a domestic cleaner since my resignation, but I'd also been trying to set up a magic business, offering myself for various events as a 'spiritual entertainer.' I've always believed that *stage* magic and *real* magic are closely connected. Not only did the former literally develop out of the latter, but stage magic also has a beautiful ability to evoke the deeper (and often long lost child-like) experience of wonder and enchantment, which is (I believe) the first necessary ingredient to living a truly magickal life.

I received an invitation, from Druid Chief Philip Carr-Gomm, to perform at the Winter Solstice Gathering of the Order of Bards, Ovates and Druids at Glastonbury. Now, because I'd always been such an eclectic and open-minded Priest, I had been reading books on modern Paganism for years and this opportunity to actually meet a few hundred of them—wow—I was over the moon. So I accepted.

[The following is an extract from my book *The Path of the Blue Raven*]

I walked into the huge Town Hall, where the Druids were assembled. It was decorated with bright and colourful banners of the various Groves, and bunches of hanging mistletoe. I took the opportunity to find Philip Carr-Gomm and introduce myself. Philip is an amazing man. He oozes genuine warmth and has a deeply spiritual air, though without any pretension or pomposity. I found him to be charming, cheerful, and welcoming. He told me what he wanted of me and I took the opportunity to get him to secretly draw me a simple picture and seal it in an envelope. I asked him to keep hold of it as I might make use of it later in my slot on stage.

It was a wonderful experience. Every performer knows when an audience is with them, and this tribe was with me. They trusted me and warmed to the message I presented. I did various mind-reading stunts, even managing to duplicate the secret drawing of the chosen chief himself! My final effect was more of a traditional magic-trick. It's how I often close a performance. I make a paper doily snow flake by cutting random holes in a folded up tissue and, as I'm doing so, talk about the symbolic nature of snow.

I left the platform with the little snowy symbols of human beauty and magic still drifting down from the ceiling. But what happened next was the real magic of the day. One after another, members of the order stepped forward to show their appreciation. I was greeted warmly when I first entered the building two hours previously. But no one knew I was a Christian vicar then. For all they knew I was a Pagan. But now they knew the truth – I was a bloody vicar! The warmth was tangible.

I stayed for the rest of the day, and well into the night, speaking to lots of members of the Order. I know I shouldn't but I can't help wondering what the welcome would have been like should the roles have been reversed. Imagine, a group of Christians are on their annual convention and they just find out that the speaker/performer is a Pagan. My hope would, of course, be that he or she be offered the same open-armed hospitality as I was, but is that realistic? I'll leave that for you to consider.

The next morning I traveled home in a daze. I'd spent the previous day and night in deep philosophical discussion but without the heavy theological debate one often finds when discussing spiritual things. The fact was that I'd felt at home there. I'd felt embraced, held, enfolded by the community—and in no sense proselytized or corrected. I had been taken for who I was. I'd even felt comfortable to share the whole story of how my life as a Vicar came to an end...*all of it*. I was listened to, accepted, and made to feel totally at home. It was genuine. That's why my head was a daze...punch-drunk on delicious Pagan hospitality.

One of the most impressive things I learned about my new friends, and their spiritual community, was that there were no set doctrines or dogmas. I even met a few other Christians there, only they were also long-term members of OBOD. I have since learned that there are OBOD Druids who are also members of almost every other religious or spiritual path. In fact there are even atheist members. It is a truly eclectic organization—which is bound to attract a good old Universalist like me.

By the time I got home I knew the encounter was not a one off. It was the beginning of something...a new phase...a new quest even! In fact it was the same quest for enchantment, but I instinctively felt I had found a new path on which to travel—as if someone had turned on the lights. I'd opened a door in a magical old wardrobe and was about to walk through.

Two years later and there I was in the cave, the Arthurian sword digging into my shoulder blade and the jagged stones piercing my knees.

After the Initiation I was given gifts from various members of the Grove and then the Druid Chief amazed me by reading me some words that had been sent especially for the occasion. Unknown to me, he (also a conjurer) had contacted my stage magic teacher from Las Vegas and told him about my initiation. My teacher replied with some beautiful words...a real gift I will never forget. This is what they said:

'Your Initiation points the way to the new spiritual road ahead of you... a road that transcends all religions. It is said that a religion is for people who are afraid of Hell. Spirituality is for people who have been there and back. Your work as a Bard is to create a sonic map; a road crafted by your words, that can lead our friends from Hell back to the Heaven that is here on Earth' ~ Jeff McBride

I'd found my path!

By Peter Nash

THIS IS A PRETTY LONG STORY, BUT HERE goes.

When I was about 14 or 15, I began to ask myself questions of a spiritual nature. I had stopped attending Church in Wales services and for a while I experimented with Eastern religions—Buddhism, Hare Krishna etc.—but they really didn't satisfy me or provide what I was looking for. Personally, I don't believe that on the whole they fit in with Western lifestyle or psyche, although of course I accept that many people in the west practice Buddhism successfully

Then—I suspect as a kind of subconscious rebellion—I made an inroad into what we would call the left-hand path. All I will say about this is that I got my fingers burned, so to speak, and it was not a pleasant experience. I soon abandoned it.

I then went away and took time out to evaluate what I really believed in. I concluded that I accepted reincarnation, at least in principle, but I was also aware that throughout nature there were complimentary opposites—night and day, black and white, spring and autumn, summer and winter etc. etc.—so therefore "god" however we perceive him/her/ it to be must reflect that. In other words, there must be a goddess as well as the god I'd heard about in church.

I was lucky enough to live just two streets away from a country park. I used to go for long walks in the woods and in amongst the trees and the stones and the plants I could feel a kind of energy, sort of like an electrical charge. The problem was I didn't know what it was or how to tap into it. I'd sometimes lie on our shed roof at night looking up at the stars and the planets. I could feel an exchange of energy with them. Again, I didn't understand why or how but I knew it was there.

One day I was browsing in a second-hand bookshop and I came across a couple of books on the Craft. Flicking through them my jaw dropped because here were all the answers—everything I'd been looking for. I bought the books and studied them with relish. I'd found my path! I really wanted to contact the authors although it didn't take me long to discover that Gerald Gardner had been dead for some 15 years.

To cut a long story short, by a strange sequence of events I got the opportunity to train with a very well-known member of the Craft, one of the biggest names in Wicca. I was initiated into the first degree on March 15th, 1982. The rest, as they say, is history...

the call of the god~dess was too great

By Rev. David R. Cobb

I GREW UP AS A BAPTIST IN NE PENNSYLVANIA, was sent into a Baptist Kindergarten, a Baptist Middle School, then a Baptist High School. Church was a big part of my life. My father was a deacon in many churches as well as a Youth Group Director. For me, the greatest gifts from this experience were 'good values and moral fortitude'. But despite all these religious influences in my life, I always felt that there was something missing.

Biblical History was one of the main topics of study throughout my earlier school years. In these classes I absorbed the stories of ancient religions especially those of the Mesopotamia River Valley, Egypt, and Sumeria, and it was because of these classes that I pursued independent study in Paganism.

In 1986 I was introduced to the *Necronomicon,* and although it has a reputation of being more of a product of fantasy than a real book of magick, it spoke loud and clear to me. I performed many rituals from the information I obtained from that little book with surprisingly great results, which spurred me on to learn more.

Later that year I was introduced to Gardnerian Witchcraft, which resulted in the establishment of a small coven. At the same time I was introduced to the ceremonial magick of the Golden Dawn. I disbanded my coven and began a full study into Ceremonialism and Rosicrucianism. Ceremonial magick, in a way, renewed my Christian beliefs. I became involved with the Pentecostal movement where I served for a brief time as a youth minister, but still could not find spiritual fulfillment.

Still, the call of the Goddess was too great. I returned to my occult studies. It wasn't until 2001 'til I found comfort and serenity and rededicated my spirituality, this time with the Correllian Nativist Tradition. I feel like now that I have aligned my soul, my dreams, and my goals with the universe, my life just seems to flow in a constant and positive direction.

I have never Looked Back

By Dyan Brown

I WAS RAISED BAPTIST AND WAS A VERY spiritual kid. I felt closest to God in the woods. I used to play alone beneath the trees...ice skating in the winter on the pond, sitting by the river under an oak tree reading in the summer. I married a Baptist man and we were very active in the church. I was a deaconess.

Two things happened to make me leave the church. One was a sermon on women who worked and how sinful that was, how they should be at home caring for their husband and children. I always have had to work to help our family survive. This was a hurtful message to be sending to those of us not economically able to live by that rule, which was nowhere in the Bible that I could find.

The other incident was that my husband was told to seek counseling because he liked children too much. He always volunteered to work in the nursery and loved playing with the kids, got down on the floor and read to them, etc. This was considered unmanly and perverted by the elders.

So we left the church and I started reading about all religions. I was an environmentalist and Wicca worshipped Mother Earth. Women were goddesses, not pawns to be ordered around by men, but strong and full of Magick. Men were allowed to be both strong and to love women and children without it seeming perverted to anyone.

I read voraciously: Green Egg, Starhawk, Raymond Buckland, Janet and Stuart Farrar, Laurie Cabot, Scott Cunningham. I met others to circle with. I fell into rhythm with the cycles of the moon and the seasons, joined a coven, and learned about perfect love and perfect trust. My art came alive with myths and symbols and my life transformed from being among the judgmental to living among free spirits.

I have never looked back. I have been a Witch for almost 40 years and my life is deeply satisfying and full of Magick.

god left me, the goddess found me

by Oisce

I FOUND TIME FOR PRAYER WHILE THE CHILD I was minding had his afternoon nap, closing my eyes, settling into the deep centre of stillness that I knew as God. I held my questions there, wanting to know what to do next, where I was meant to be. I had left the convent, not through any crisis of faith, rather, because of faith. I wanted to live a radical lifestyle of devotion to God but had instead found myself ensconced in middle-class prosperity while working with homeless kids, women in prison and and streetworkers. The gulf was too great.

But in leaving the convent, I had also left the people on the streets, and I did want to keep working with them. So where to next? I took time out to come back to my family home while I waited on direction from God. Every day I went to mass, received communion, every evening read the Office, the regulated prayers set out in the breviary, every day found time to sit in the silence of God and wait on his direction.

This day, it came. When I talk about hearing the voice of God, it is not like an auditory hallucination booming through the walls. Rather, it is a knowing, a hearing inside. I heard God say he was leaving and I would have to find him in a new way. And then he left. Just left.

I had known the presence of God all my life. Now, for the first time when I reached in, there was nothing there. When I reached out, there was nothing there. When I received communion, there was nothing, like a reverse transubstantiation from the Body of Christ into a tasteless, soul-less, dry bit of paper-thin bread. Still, I went through the motions, went to Mass, read my Office, said the rosary, waiting for God to return. Trusting that God would return.

A week after God left me, my brother died, hit by a train. It felt like I had been hit by the train. As the religious one, it fell to me to organise the church funeral, and I attended to every detail, choosing songs and readings that would bring some meaning to my wild brother's life, to his death. But the priest would not allow my brother's music, said it was four-four beat and the devil's music (church music is three-four). I argued the case, burst into tears, won that victory. But when my brother's mates turned up to check out the PA system, the priest did not like the look of them and took it away. They still played, but no one could hear them.

I was anointed as a special minister of the Eucharist, which meant I could give communion. I had not planned to, because I was there as a grieving sister, but I went up and stood beside the priest knowing that my brother's non-Catholic friends would come to me. I gave them communion and then, when I walked out that sandstone church, I walked out of the Church. If my brother and his friends were not good enough for the church, the church was not good enough for me.

I walked out of the church and off the cliff, into the void, a bottomless dark limbo with no thread to hang onto, no glimmer of light, no soothing, easing, healing presence of the God who had always loved me. Jesus, I ranted, how could you abandon me at this time? I did not understand, did not understand anything about life, had no frame of reference for understanding anything.

But I found work with the street kids and they kept me going, gave me a reason to keep going. And with no restriction on purity or celibacy or need for marriage now, just human sexuality, I also found a lover. He introduced me to the tarot. I had always regarded the tarot, anything occult, to be evil, the devil's work, because only God could help your divine your pathway. But God was gone. And the tarot was so damned accurate. I started to read, found I had an aptitude for it. It wasn't God's voice, nothing I recognized. I thought maybe it was my own. There was still the void but I had learned to ignore it and spent more time looking outward than in.

When we were made redundant from our jobs, we moved into a plain farmhouse, not even a farmhouse. It was a modified building shifted from an immigration camp. But it suited our needs. Time on my hands, I thought I would try gardening. First, I started the seeds on cotton wool, then when they began to sprout, I moved them into little pots, and then into the garden beds, carefully, like they were children. I fed, watered, weeded as they grew into flowers, herbs and vegetables. Inexplicably, the void started to subside, ease away. I gardened more, planted more, got to know the plants, their likes and dislikes, their healing properties. They began to heal me.

Then, the strangest thing. The Goddess came looking for me. She was everywhere I turned. I would pick up a magazine at the doctor's and there would be an article on Her, on a Pagan group that honoured Her as the Great Mother. I read a Mills and Boon where the female protagonist was a witch. Books jumped out at me, *Good Magic* by Marina Medici. I studied crystals as well as herbs, started paying attention to the natural cycles. Everywhere I turned, there She was. I could feel her presence as I walked barefoot on the soft earth, swam in the living river, let the rays of the moon wash over me, or the sun warm my flesh. I could feel her there when I wrote and when I made love and when I cooked and when I gardened. Always there.

I found Shekhinah Mountainwater's *Ariadne's Thread* and began following the transformative course she laid out, learning to listen to the Mother's voice as I walked on the land. There was no more void, there was She, a sense of coming home, home to myself to the land, to the Mother. At the start of the course, I laid out an altar. When I finished thirteen lunar cycles later, I unpacked that altar and moved out to begin a new life dedicated to the Goddess.

But what of the God who had fathered me, Christ who had died for me, ressurrected and walked alongside me? Years on, a fully fledged Pagan, I was at the pub one night having a long drunken conversation with an old friend from youth group days. We were talking about the Church, how it had become more important to him with his own family. He couldn't believe that I, who had been so religious, had left.

"Nah, once a Catholic, always a Catholic," he said to me.

I told him the church would not have me if they knew what I was.

"Nah, once a Catholic, always a Catholic."

All the following week, it played over and over in my mind like a mantra until that next Sunday, when I found myself walking back into that same sandstone church I had walked out following my brother's funeral. I nodded at old acquaintances, still seemed to know many of the people there, I joined in the prayers and responses, and when I went up to receive communion, the Body of Christ, it felt like I was meeting an old and beloved friend again. Comfortable, easy, okay.

I had moved on, was a different person. My old God had left me and I had found God in a new way, in Mother Earth, and that was as it was meant to be. She had gathered me up and carried me home. But every now and then, I can visit my old God, like visiting an old friend, and thank him for having the love and wisdom to leave me so I would find instead my own way, and that way led me home, home to Mother.

Oisce is the magical name of an Australian writer and poet who has had a variety of work published, including Sunwyse: Celebrating the Wheel of the Year in Australia. *Her interest in religion and spirituality has seen her explore many world views, but it is the path of Earth-based spirituality she has chosen to walk. That walk led her to Ireland where she explored her heritage, learned about folk wisdom, the oral art of storytelling, and danced with the fairies. Back in Australia, living on Bangerang country, she is a sheep-farmer, a poet with a PhD, and a religious (Pagan) and civil celebrant for weddings and funerals.*

I Should Bake Cookies

By Stanley M. Nowakowski Jr.

WAS RAISED IN THE CATHOLIC CHURCH. I remember the lying to the priest in the confessional. But I received first communion, and confirmation. I drifted from the church just after my 18th birthday, November 1977.

In 1986, when I was nearing the nadir of my drug and alcohol abuse, I was writing to my parish priest. We had a dialogue. I wrote letters to him, and he would reply during his sermons. I got clean and sober in November of 1986 and continued my communication with the priest.

All was well until Easter Sunday. He let loose a fire and brimstone sermon. It was mostly dealing with sexual behavior. When the congregation went forward to receive communion, I walked out the back door.

By August I found a copy of a Paul Huson book on Witchcraft. I jumped in with both feet.

There were some idyllic years. The study of Witchcraft led me to Tarot. The study of Tarot led me to Kabbalah. And Kabbalah led me back to Christ. But I'm far from being a Catholic. I look on the Christ as a manifestation of the dying and resurrected vegetation God.

I see the Universe not as an artifact that was constructed by a male divinity, but as a living being that was given birth to by a female divinity.

I consider myself "Christopagan." I have learned things about the World that don't fit into the Christian mythos as it is presented today. I never threw Jesus away when I looked to the Goddess. Nor have I abandoned the Goddess looking back to Christ.

I received two visitations by the Christ. I try to live my life by what he presented to me on those occasions. One... Homosexuality is not only permitted, but when sexual gifts are shared freely and appropriately, they are to be rewarded... and... Two... I should bake cookies.

BReaking thROUGh

By Drena Griffe

Like waking up from the longest dream
How real it seemed
Until Your love broke through

I've been lost in a fantasy
That blinded me
Until Your love broke through

"Your Love Broke Through" ~ Keith Green

IT MAY SEEM STRANGE TO BEGIN AN ESSAY about leaving Jesus for the Goddess by quoting Christian song lyrics. Ironically, I truly came to recognize the Love in these verses after walking away from the Christian path. But I'm getting a bit ahead of myself.

My transition from Christianity to Paganism did not happen easily. I grew up Catholic in the Coastal South. My parents weren't particularly religious, but sent my brother and me to Catholic school, so twice weekly church attendance was required. My dad never attended, and my mom and brother attended ambivalently. However, I loved it! I loved the ritual and liturgy, ongoing gestures of devotion and connection. I remember gazing longingly at the veiled "Handmaids of Mary," a group of girls devoted to our Blessed Mother. But, if I'm being honest, my young faith was based more on an idea than the reality of my life.

There was a lot about myself and my life that I didn't know at the time – for instance, that my maternal grandmother had converted to Catholicism in the hopes of sending her youngest children to the newly-integrated Catholic high school.

My mother was the only POC in her graduating class, and she actively carried the pain of isolation and social rejection, which I now believe partly fueled her religious antipathy. However, my mother's side of the family prioritized education above other concerns. Even though I was unusually devoted by their standards, my childhood faith was simply a means to an end.

Ironically, racial politics played an active role in my school life as well. I had grown up sitting at my grandmother's feet, actively taking in the family stories which included tales of black, white and indigenous ancestors. I believed I could be related to the entire world, and endeavoured to meet everyone with kindness and openness. But just two decades after my mother's journey through the same Catholic school, the environment was still segregated in spirit. I remember being called the n-word, and ridiculed regularly. Also, strangely to my mind, I was ostracized from the few other non-white students as well. Unbeknownst to me, word had gotten around that I was somehow different from all others.

These weren't the only contradictions coloring my young religious experience.

My mother was emotionally and physically abusive. As a child I internalized her anger and rejection, whereas my brother, precocious and highly gifted, acted out. Years later he confessed that one of our teachers, a nun, once spoke with him privately about the abuse. She told him how strong he was, but for whatever reason declined to actively intervene.

I also remember several kindly teachers taking an interest in me and providing me some shelter while at school. At the time I was just grateful for the acceptance and brief respite and didn't consider any implications beyond that. I've reconstructed these painful details of my young life slowly, over many decades, as part of my own journey towards inner healing. As an adult I gathered the insight to grapple with the family pathology around race and abuse. Only now am I able to see that my mother's abusive behavior was fueled by a secret she had been keeping that would in time impact me more profoundly than any other experience I would ever have.

With such an unstable life, my early religious devotion makes sense. Yet I, too, had a secret of my own.

I honestly cannot tell you when I began hearing the inner voice; somewhere around the age of six, I think. What I more easily recall are the bouts with insomnia juxtaposed with periods of intense dreaming. The inner voice often kept me awake at night, made me restless, and didn't often have a lot of positive things to say about our situation. Initially I feared it, thinking I should shut it off or at least turn down its volume. But eventually, like other aspects of my life I had no choice but to learn to live with it. Rarely and unbidden, it would offer some unique insight.

When I was sixteen, we studied holy orders in religion class and I remember being deeply drawn to the path of the cloistered monk. I was seriously considering it until the voice said:

Are you doing this because you love God or because you're afraid of people?

"Well...I do love God...but I'm definitely afraid of people."

Not a good enough reason to take a vow.

So I didn't. But that was one of the few times I listened without defense. For all of my many regrets about my early religious years, I sincerely wish that I had cultivated a relationship with my inner voice instead of treating it like an outcast. I wish that I had named it instead of silencing it almost to death. But I didn't. I was a daughter of the church to the exclusion of my own humanity.

For many people the deconstruction of faith comes after a period of intense scrutiny and/or running headlong into the inherent hypocrisy in some of the church's moral teachings. In my case, I was too worn from fighting so many battles! With such an unstable home and fragile inner life, the church formed my moral center due to being the only stable and compassionate element I'd experienced. In moments of rising doubt, especially around key social issues, I had been conditioned to question myself rather than my faith.

So how did I break free? I don't think I would have ever left the church on my own. It honestly came down to geographic circumstance: I attended college away from home. My hometown and surrounding area is predominantly Catholic, but the community where I first attended college was Southern Baptist. Naively I attended services at the campus Baptist Student Union, and I had no idea that there were different ways of being Christian. (Weren't we all the same?) I also had no idea that as a Catholic I was seen by many Baptists as "unsaved" and ripe for the spiritual picking!

I've heard a lot of people lament that the Catholic church taught them the meaning of shame. While I can see how that might be the case, for me it was the Baptists! Initially I fell for the "salvation" narrative because, still the wounded daughter, I thought it might help me fashion myself into someone my mother could love. Of course this did not happen, but the grueling expectations created a spiritual standard that no matter how hard I strove I could never meet.

This spiritual community was as racially separated as the Catholic school I attended. Though I did encounter a few kindhearted people, mostly I endured veiled prejudice: when a

young man from the local homeless shelter visited our church, I
befriended him and invited him to dinner. My intention had been to
share the love of Christ, but the ladies of the church gossiped about
me. "You can't take the slut out of that kind!" Not a single person
stepped aside to say, "As a young woman, you need to be careful."
I didn't consider that I might be putting myself in any sort of danger,
just as I didn't consider that when I picked up strangers to offer them
rides or randomly stopped to give water and cold drinks to strangers
baking in the southern sun. I believed that, as a Christian, it was my
duty to spread Christ's love. I had long stopped expecting to receive
love in return.

I'd like to say that I wised up quickly, but in truth it took about
ten years for me to finally leave. In the end I was broken by an
inability to live up to the standards set for me as a Christian. It was
the almost boyfriend, a wannabe minister who said that he'd rejected
me even though he had feelings for me because he "didn't want to
have interracial babies who would suffer." It was the heartbroken
friend who stopped talking to me after my "judgmental" response to
her abortion. It was the summer spent working with missionaries
who were relieved of their duties after allowing homeless people to
sleep on the floor of the shelter after hours. Finally, it was the
recognition that my so-called faith didn't line up with reality, and
had never lined up with the truth of my life as it was.

But where to next? I had only ever known Christianity; I had
nowhere else to turn, and didn't trust myself. At first I thought
maybe I should just give up belief entirely. That lasted for about two
minutes. In moments of quiet, I could sense, even feel, a thread of
recognition running all throughout my life. In the midst of the early
pain, I had also been protected by something, or someone. If I got
very still, I could even feel the stirrings of that inner voice, long
silenced and nearly strangled, but still alive and willing to come
back to work with me. It understood, perhaps better than I did, that
in moments of desperation sometimes we turn against ourselves. But
we do it in order to survive. When we know better, we can learn to
make better, more empowering choices. First we have to learn to
value ourselves.

During the earlier years of my deconstruction of faith, a former
Christian friend advised me, "Leave the church if you must, but
don't leave Christ."

But in the quietude I cultivated in those initial months and years after leaving the church, the one I didn't sense was Jesus or the Christian God. I could still feel lingering guilt and shame, but not any love. Looking back, I realized that what had bound me to these beings was guilt and shame all along.

Finally listening to my inner stirrings, I turned to the indigenous path, in part due to the childhood stories and a desire for a worldview of shared spiritual kinship.

In a shamanic journey, I experienced the following:

I am naked, standing near a pool of water in the forest. Darkness is all around me, except the light from the full moon above the pool. I am instructed to get into the pool and am attended to by invisible hands. After bathing and submerging in the sacred pool, I rise and am dressed in a flowing white gown. There is an archway to the left and a path winding deeper and deeper into the darkness. I know this is the path I must follow. I have been chosen—claimed—by the Goddess. I will know times of darkness. At times I will feel deeply alone. But I am Love and Loved. I now have a path. And this path will lead me Home.

It's been nearly fifteen years since that fateful inner journey. Since then, it's been my experience that the Goddess wears many faces depending upon the need. I could write another 2,000 words and still not scratch the surface of Her. She is fierce and protective. She is wise. She is bold. She is unapologetic. Above all else, She keeps Her Word.

This snapshot of my spiritual journey is far from complete. But I'd like to close by saying that while I have lingering grief about my time as a Christian, I don't regret it. The Goddess has taught me that it's important to embrace everything as part of the gift of being human. While I don't believe that bad things happen for a reason, I believe that even our deepest pain can be catalyzed, redeemed and called into the service of Love.

Drena Griffe is a minister of Incarnational Spirituality and spiritual companion. She embodies an eclectic practice drawing from deep inner wells, as well as a series of multifaceted religious and spiritual traditions. Drena can be reached at pilgrimatthecrossroads.com or drena.griffe@gmail.com.

the puzzle piece I'd been missing

By Rev. Mel J Fleming II

MY STORY BEGINS AS A TORTURED child survivor of the Catholic Church. They had the only school in my area. They were brutal. They beat children for the slightest inference of even questioning their authority. They were quite expert and thorough in the deviate castigation inflicted upon children.

The headman there was Rev. Leo T. McGovern, a wolf in sheep's clothing if there ever was one. There are horror films that easily mirror him; in fact, watching; "American Horror Story, The Asylum," comes close. He was man who thrilled in physically, emotionally, and sexually tormenting children. For many years I suffered greatly from him, the nuns, and some of these "godly" school children, who knew nothing else but to express their pain through that of others.

After secondary form, my desire was to escape all forms of Catholicism. I wasn't sure what I was seeking. My Catholic fanatic step-mum, Dorothy died. I was more than happy to see her buried and shed no tears, despite her being ravaged with lung cancer. Her abuse, both physical and emotional, left such scars upon my mind and heart that the memories are still intact and searing in the present time. However, I made a decision that proved to be another grave error.

I was befriended by the local evangelicals from a Bible college who literally beguiled me with friendship and a sense of community. A year later I was enrolled, taking classes, and learning the dogmas of Pentecostal-originated Christianity. That was near the beginning of the end.

Two years after seeing the hypocrisy of both staff and students, I left, seeking employment. However, instead of leaving Christianity, I became once again embroiled in the faith with a mixed sense of commitment. I often rebelled against what I perceived as dogma, which was not so much scripturally supported but the personal interpretation of the leadership. This was during the time when groups such as the Moral Majority with Jerry Falwell, Focus on the Family, the organization headed by James Dobson, and others infiltrated the Christian evangelical movement. I was under constant pressure to alter my social and political beliefs, especially in the churches I'd attended. I was pro-choice, had gay, lesbian and trans-gendered friends. I was in civil rights groups that my church leadership disapproved of. I was involved in protecting women's health clinics against anti-abortion groups such as Operation Rescue, headed by Randall Terry. These encounters were often quite violent, as we delivered patients through hostile crowds determined to stop entrance at all costs. Here I was, an evangelical, physically fighting off others of my faith, sometimes violently, so women could have safe access to clinical care.

Was I ashamed, or felt guilty? Not in the least. In my mind, the only one to judge them was "God" himself. Too many times to mention had I received critical review due to my stances, because many of these people represented a form of Christianity my paternal elders opposed. Their stances on issues, and civil rights and liberties, were the very thing my minister, his wife, and my father marched against. Yet in this new evangelical movement I was literally being pounded on these issues on a regular basis. However I withstood the arguments, responding that the scriptures they used in opposition were in no way in correlation and easily misconstrued to suit politicization of the bible.

I was independently ordained at the time, outside of the church. There were other evangelicals who held to the same political and social beliefs I'd expressed. In fact, they're still in existence. However, the pressure was so great that I decided I needed to close the book on Christianity, and if it were true that I'd end up in hell, that was my problem, not theirs.

I would have felt justified to point a finger at Jesus and yell, "Really? Send me to hell; what about them? Do something about them before you condemn me. Where the hell were you, when I was a child, being abused by the priests and nuns, all those damned years? You're supposed to be the true God and you've no control over your followers? As a God you're a deadbeat dad."

I became a Pagan quite strangely. In 1992 I was walking by a "medieval and historical" bookstore in Riverside, California, named The DragonMarsh. Curiously, I walked in, perusing the book section, when I happened upon *Wicca, a Guide for the Solitary Practitioner* by Scott Cunningham. I bought that book and several others and took them home. The message in the book struck home, and I immediately sensed this was the major puzzle piece I'd been missing in my life. I began scouring the shop for even more materials, asking questions, meeting other Pagans, Wiccans, and Witches, which served only to enhance my practices. Through the years I attended seminars, had involvement in Covens, groups, and continued to develop my own unique and eclectic path.

Since that time it's still been a tough road, with many bumps and rough edges. However, in contrast to my former years, I'd not trade them for anything. Even now, I still suffer from the memories and have trust issues. Even to this day I discover Pagans who are close to those Catholics and Evangelicals. I simply avoid them.

hail, holy queen of heaven

by Jim "Raven" Stefanowicz

VE MARIA, GRATIA PLENA, DOMINUS Tecum. Those were the words that danced from the mouths of the parishioners at Sacred Heart of Jesus Church on a sunny May morning in 2001. In English tongue, the words translate to, "Hail Mary, full of grace, the Lord is with you," the first few words of one of the most uttered prayers in Catholicism. They were written to honor Mary, Mother of Jesus Christ, and I was only 8 years old when I first spoke them. Having recently been enrolled in Sacred Heart of Jesus Parochial School, I would come to know them well.

My South Philadelphia upbringing was nestled in the loving hands of my Roman Catholic family who, while not as devout as some of our neighbors, had received all their sacraments of initiation and attended Mass most Sundays. In an attempt to adhere to the expectations placed on Catholic parents at the time, my mother and grandparents saved the money needed to enroll me in parochial school. It was in the autumn of the year 2000 that my studies within the walls of Sacred Heart of Jesus School began. In those days, Catholic schools were thought superior, undoubtedly a remnant of the Church's sanctimonious attitude about non-Catholic institutions. Those parents who enrolled their children in public school (usually out of financial necessity) were viewed by the community as being religiously and morally negligent.

Every day at school felt like a lengthy church service. The school's principal was a nun—as were most of the teachers—and religion was king of curriculum. Instead of Evolution, we were told of a garden with a tree, an apple, two humans, a snake, and an unforgiveable sin. The only thing missing was a partridge in a pear tree. And instead of human rights, the Sisters taught us every book of the Old Testament in their order of appearance. We prayed the entire rosary weekly during Sister Andrew's Religious Enrichment and attended school Masses monthly. These did not count towards the weekend and family Mass we were also expected to attend. Inability to attend would sometimes result in detention.

During my time as a student at Sacred Heart, I received the sacraments of Reconciliation, Communion, and Confirmation, which was mandatory. Outside of the school's walls I was a member of the Archdiocesan Boys Choir of Philadelphia, a traveling choir that consisted of boys from some of the city's Catholic schools, and frequently performed in churches and cathedrals all over the East Coast. This led to Sacred Heart's assistant pastor, Father Dean, asking me to work at the church as a cantor, a post I would hold for more than 20 years—16 of which were after my conversion to Paganism.

As the years passed, I became increasingly disconnected from the archaic Catholic dogma that polluted the minds of my peers. I hated the idea of a God whose demands are rooted in fear of the things that would come to pass should one not obey him. I did not see the value in confessing one's darkest secrets to an appointed commissary in an attempt at third-party forgiveness. And I certainly did not agree with the Bible being weaponized to defend views that lacked morality.

Having known I was gay for most of my life, the Gospels brought me no peace, and the Church's disgusting views on homosexuality brought me no warmth. Sacred Heart's neo-gothic architecture, while always beautiful, was also always cold to me. This was because I knew the secrets that dwelled within its walls. Their names were judgment, homophobia, bigotry, racism, ignorance, and subservience, and their roots ran deep. Over time I came to realize that the beatitude, "Blessed are the Poor in Spirit," was actually "Blessed are the Rich in Pocket." "Grace" had become something one could buy, and something only few could afford.

So how did I find the Goddess? There is a reason I began my story with Mary. In the years surrounding my forced descent into the dark cavern of Christianity, Mary had always been a constant and guiding light. She was a Divine Woman in a world of misogynistic men. And because I was fortunate enough in my childhood to be raised by strong women, Mary was the only Christian deity that I could really relate to. She was loving, forgiving, and everything a mother should be.

Having frequently watched the film adaptation of Marion Zimmer Bradley's *The Mists of Avalon*, I was well aware of who Mary really was. Not some subservient lesser deity, but the Mother Goddess herself, crowned in wisdom and robed in the Sun. Through honoring her in her true form, the doorway to the Old Ways opened itself to me. I began to see things through a lens of truth. In the Eucharistic Rite, I saw the Dionysian Mysteries. In the Holy Days of Obligation, I saw the Sabbats. The list began to grow. And while I did not know the proper names mentioned above at the time, I felt their truths. While I never heard a voice in the beginning calling me home (to Paganism) in a soft whisper like some other people I know, the compass of my heart pointed me in that direction. And I know that it was the Goddess who calibrated it. The Goddess accepted me for who I was, and that was something I desperately needed.

When I first ventured into Paganism, there was not really a strong Pagan community in Philly. MySpace—while ancient now—was the best way to interact with followers of the Old Religion. I was online constantly operating under the magickal name, Dragon Walker. I would scroll through Pagan profiles, absorbing all the information I possibly could, while all the while private messaging those whose profiles I most resonated with. Though virtual, I really felt as if I had finally found a tribe.

Then in 2004, my stepfather at the time gifted me a copy of *Grimoire for the Apprentice Wizard*. The book not only saved my life by bringing validity to the concepts and practices that I came to view as personal truths, but it also provided me with my first solid intro to Paganism. It was not long after that time when that same stepfather (Tommy) would take me shopping at Harry's Occult Shop, a Philadelphia staple, and the oldest occult shop in the country (operating for over 100 years until closing). I was not old enough at the time to go shopping there alone, so Tommy would take me weekly, buying the candles, oils, incenses, and herbs I needed for the spells and rituals I was performing at the time. When I came out of the broom closet to my immediate family, they did not have much to say. While I was met with the ever immortalized, "you're not worshipping the devil, are you?" my family saw how fulfilled I was. And that was something they prioritized over all else. My Grandmother—arguably the most devout Catholic in my immediate family—even came to ask me for money candles every now and again.

While they had never been interested in the details, my family respected my spirituality for what it was—mine.

My first in-person training came at the hands of a Christian lightworker named Lisa. She was a gifted clairvoyant and an extremely experienced astrologist. Above all, she was one of the fiercest mothers I have ever known, and eventually became a second mother to me. I remember the first time I walked into her room like it was yesterday. The warm aroma of frankincense filled the air, and metaphysical books—as numerous as the stars—graced each wall.

Lisa had already heard of my coming out of the broom closet before I arrived at her house that day, so when I looked at her face, I saw pure love looking back at me.

Lisa had always been private about her spiritual practice, out of fear of judgment from her Christian family and friends, even until the end. During Lisa's childhood years—when her abilities started to surface—her Catholic mother put her into a mental institution as a way of suppressing her abilities. The strength of Lisa's determination could not be dimmed however, and she continued to grow her abilities and practice her craft in secret.

A gifted healer, Lisa eventually became an ER Nurse, a post she held until her passing. She incorporated many Christian facets into her practice, proving to me that the Christianity could be as positive or as toxic as the person walking it, and she really embodied the best of Christ's qualities. This Goddess incarnate was instrumental in my spiritual growth, and her indomitable spirit taught me that it is better to live a solitary life in truth, than to be surrounded by smiling faces rooted in a lie. She was a true example of what it means to endure, and I will forever be grateful to her. May her memory be as eternal as her love.

Today, I am a Pagan Priest and Witch with not an ounce of Christianity in my practice. While I believe that Jesus Christ was a prophet and skilled magician, I do not believe him to be a God in the omnipotent sense. I worship the Old Gods and practice the Ancient Ways. I am an initiate in the Ash, Birch, and Willow tradition of Witchcraft, and I also hold a second degree within the Cabot Kent Hermetic Temple. I am the High Priest and founder of the South Street Circle, a Pagan ritual group that meets during the Sabbats in Philadelphia, and I have led public rituals in Philly including at Philadelphia Pagan Pride Day. As pagan clergy, I have performed handfasting rituals, baby blessings, house cleansings, and other rites when called upon. I own and operate, Mandragora: A Witch Shop, and until recently, managed the newer incarnation of Harry's Occult Shop—the store I mentioned earlier. I am a professional tarot reader—certified through the Cabot Academy of Witchcraft—and I am also proficient at reading the Elder Futhark Runes, and Stones. In Philadelphia, I am one of the more public figures in the Pagan community and strive each day to be a positive representation of what it means to be a Witch.

To all of you reading this who walk the path of Christianity, I have these things to say to you:

- Do not condemn others in the name of your God—his law is love.
- Do not allow a priest to speak for your God—your God will speak to you.
- Do not forsake your personal truths in the name of an outdated book—your God did not write it.
- Do not try to buy your way into heaven—grace cannot be bought.
- Do not pass judgment—your God condemns it.
- Do not look for your God in hatred—he does not dwell there.
- Do not think you are unworthy of love—you were made from it.
- Do not fear sin—fear is a sin.
- Do not allow yourselves to become lost in pursuit of your God—he already resides within you.
- Love one another, as your God loves you.

Raven Shadowhawk

my journey from catholicism to pachamama

By Rev. Jacqueline "Omi" Zaleski Mackenzie, Ph.D.

In the Beginning:

MY RIGID AMERICAN SYNOD Lutheran/ Roman Catholic religious upbringing was via my devout father's influence. The only aspect of stability within my transient military-dependent childhood was visiting a church. By third grade, I had moved 23 times while living in 23 different U.S. States, but my parents made sure that I never missed church, Sunday School, choir practice, or Brownie Scouts. All my social or religious activities took place in a church somewhere inside the United States.

My Religious Training:

My father, raised Roman Catholic, was dedicated to my religious education; when he was home (less than 50% of the time), he took me to church. When he was away on military missions, some other military adult took me to church. My mother, who was raised Lutheran, rarely attended church functions. I was baptized and confirmed in the American Synod of the Lutheran Church, but my domestic religious training inside our home was Roman Catholic.

During puberty, I attended catechism classes. Every summer I participated in a church-sponsored camp. At barely fifteen years old (1962), after being raped and impregnated I was sent to a Roman Catholic nunnery for eight months.

I'd rate my religious upbringing as having devoutly motivated religious demands with poor adult mentoring when my father was absent.

My Parents:

My parents were very mismatched and also estranged from both of their families. My father, who was very dark skinned, was only

5' 6" tall. His parents were Polish immigrants into the U.S. He was disowned by his strict Roman Catholic family due to marrying my mother. My mother, who was extremely fair-skinned—her nickname was "Cameo"—was of Scotch/Irish descent. She was 6' 1" tall and the niece of a Lutheran minister.

In August 1940 at ages 25 (Dad) and 21 (Mother), they married, just 28 days after meeting each other. The story is that they married so soon because they both wanted children, specifically six tall sons. Yet after years of trying, there was no pregnancy.

In 1945, right after serving in WWII, my father left the Army Air Corps to run a small subsistence farm in Roswell, New Mexico. That's where Mother finally became pregnant. I was born in early 1947, shortly before a reported landing of an alien spaceship near our farm. (My father visited that "alien" site and reported what he saw and had touched.)

Eighteen months after I was born, my mother gave birth to a boy, six weeks past his due date. An Rh negative baby, he lived only four days. Thus, I was raised as an only child and in my mother's eyes unwanted.

My father was was recalled into the Army Air Corps under a Top Secret clearance. He always said it happened because of what he saw in Roswell.

I received little input from my absent father other than occasional letters.

Conversations with God:

I have fought feelings of guilt my entire life because I was not born male. I felt shame that my Mother so hated me. I felt inadequate in that I was not able to transform into a male. For most of my childhood, I asked God, "Why was I born female?" I tried over and over again to pray my way into a male body so that I'd be loved. I also prayed to not be beaten.

Thus, my crisis of faith came early. I constantly asked, "Why me? What have I done? Where is God?"

Restrictions via Religious Doctrine:

My conflict with the church's teachings was related to a lack of expressions of love, trust, honesty, sex education, and basic kindness. Those qualities were especially absent from my disabled,

lonely, miserable and alcoholic mother. There was less of such behavior from my father because he was rarely home.

I was married and moved from my parents by age 16.

Religious Doctrines Studied:

Early on, I studied religious differences due to the upheaval that
fact caused in my family. Jesus was not a significant player in the
line-up of my religious training. Throughout my entire youth, my
idea of Jesus was as a prophet. Yes, he was called the son of God,
but he was not God.

After the hypocrisy that I saw in the nunnery, I ran from both
Lutheran and Roman Catholic teachings. On my own, I studied var-
ious Pagan-labeled spiritual pathways. By 1963 I had explored
Renzi Zen Buddhism, Hinduism and was active in Unitarian Uni-
versalist (UU) churches. I was committed to running one Unitarian
Universalist Sunday School and several UU retreats with children.

Discovering Mother Earth: Pachamama

The concept of a Divine Female was woven into my father's Roman Catholic influences. I always imagined a Divine Female would
"save" me. It was not until 1990 that I called Her "Goddess." Then,
I *fell totally in love* with the concept of "Goddess" as equal to God.

As a Postulant, I Vowed a Life of Service to Mother Earth:

In Jacksonville, Florida, I studied North European Shamanism
under woman named Kathy and her gay male teaching partner, Harold Powell. I deeply admired and respected Harold's knowledge, be-
haviors, outlook on the Pagan lifestyle, and teaching style. I took
any academic crumbs I could get from Harold.

I left that group after a dispute with Karen. In other groups I was
exposed to various teachers within Florida. In January 1991, I became a student under Rt. Rev. Pete Pathfinder Davis, founder of The
Aquarian Tabernacle Church; I was his student for over 20 years. I
have been ordained Clergy in ATC, Asatru, UUB and more to aid in
being able to make volunteer prison visitations. I loved helping in
any manner possible; I still do.

Early Clergy Challenges While in Service to Mother:

I learned what my commitment to serve Mother Earth actually meant when I took a public stand over a four-year period for the right to worship in a home,

My spouse Roger, friends and I were "guilty" of worshiping with a few friends outside in a one-acre rural yard. Two doors away, the then vice president of the Mormon Church frequently held large outdoor events in his same-sized rural backyard, and had for many years. His events were ignored. Ours often had TV cameras over our garage roof pointed into our back yard sacred circle.

The person who started the entire series of legal events was "horrified" that I was of Polish heritage and yet did not attend "her" local Roman Catholic Church. She belonged to the same congregation as the City Planning and Zoning Manager and convinced him to notify us via a government letter that if we (five people or fewer; including family members) worshiped on our property—even a blessing during a birthday party—we would be fined $500 a day for every day from that day forward regardless if we were worshiping on a day or not! My husband. and I had no choice but to take a legal stand against the City of Palm Bay, Florida.

Within a few weeks our story had thousands of hits on the less than a decade old Internet. We were featured on the front page of the local Palm Bay Florida newspaper (far too often), on CNN News, in a newspaper in the UK and on the cover of the Miami Herald Sunday Magazine.

As a result, up to 765 phone calls a day came into my home. They included three or four death threats a month, primarily from fundamentalist Christians.

On Samhain (October 31st) I testified at the Palm Bay City Council. There was a significant uproar. All over the city, people gathered in homes for the event which had been advertised in church bulletins from a multitude of denominations.

Later, I gave the invocation (a religious blessing), for the opening of a Titusville City Council Meeting. Over 200 people packed the second-floor room, the first floor, and outside the building, the largest turnout ever. As soon as I uttered the first sound, all 200+ people screamed out "The Lord's Prayer." As I left the building, I was verbally confronted by the mob.

In 1994, my current husband, Donald James Mackenzie,and I traveled the US speaking on "Religious Freedom is for All Religions."

We finally had our day in court at the U.S. District Court of Florida on October 11, 1994. We won![44] But there were significant costs: $60,000 in legal fees, our marriage, my job, my home and my reputation as a sensible person. I was the public face both in Florida and the other 49 states.

My experiences with The Church of Iron Oak, A.T.C. connected me with who I am. I never looked back in my four-year legal battle for religious freedom for Wicca. I have continued to grow and expand my love of the Goddess. For 20+ years, Pete Pathfinder was always there for me, teaching, coaching, commenting, and encouraging; he was supportive until just before his death.

I have also come to terms with this fact: "You are special to your God, not My God, but your God." That phrase was said to me in 1992 when a gasoline pump that exploded did not kill me. I never forgot the sweet old black grandmother who was holding her granddaughter's hand. She saw how I barely missed death that day.

My pathway is Earth-Centered Pagan, through and through, to my last breath.

I went on the continue to worship Mother Earth with the most committed level as a deep ecologist. Don Mackenzie and I backed our U.S. nonprofit, Summerland Monastery, with our own personal guarantees. We bought 1,227 acres of high desert land named Wind-Tree Ranch. We created a Pagan Eco-Retreat Center before Y2K and stayed afterward. We built fourteen eco-friendly dwellings: dry composting toilets, water wells, no zoning restrictions, and self-sufficient. We housed about 11 residents and many visitors, and taught 100 about various forms of eco-friendly building and living styles.

In May 2008, we moved to Central Mexico and managed programs for marginally compromised indigenous children. In 2009 and 2010, we oversaw the building of a community center for these children and their families.

Later Clergy Challenges While in Service to Mother:

In 2013, Pete Pathfinder pushed me out of the ATC with the stunning words, "Stop teaching Mexicans; Wiccan lessons are only for Northern Europeans."

I had been living in Central Mexico, at least part of the year, since 2005, permanently in an indigenous village since 2008. To

---

[44] https://law.justia.com/cases/federal/district-courts/FSupp/868/1361/2149005/

obey that command left me with no coven. So, I left ATC. and followed my husband's pathway to the Church of All Words (CAW) where my husband had been for decades. Within CAW, I found the doctrines that best suited my soul then and now.

In 2013, we moved to Ecuador to clean air, pure water, and a life—once again—entirely devoted to honoring our Mother Earth.

We now live in an Eco-Hobbit House that we built. The homestead, on leased land, is off the power grid. We are working toward self-sustainability. In August of 2019 we were thrilled to share our joy here with a visit from Oberon Zell-Ravenheart and his traveling companion. While he was here, he ordained me as a high priestess of CAW. What an honor!

Recent Clergy Challenges:

I continue to serve CAW in whatever ways are needed and approved as my respect for CAW and many other Pagans and non-conventional organizations have not waned.

I feel blessed to have found the only Mother I need or have ever needed spiritually. With Her as my Goddess, I looked deeper, more comprehensively, and with no reservations regarding who I am, what value I have, how She is helping me, and who She is. I now know that service to Her in every man, woman, or child has always been and will always be my calling. I wish that you will also find the stability that I have found for not only yourself but also for all those with whom you come into contact, regardless of the reasons, goals, or conversations.

Jacqueline "Omi" Zaleski Mackenzie has been an ordained minister since 1994, a nonprofit administrator continuously since 1986, and an advocate for organic farming since 1972. "Omi" is also an educator, social scientist, and author of 14 books. Specializing in Business Systems Management for nonprofits, she earned her M.S. and B.S. from the Florida Institute of Technology. She later earned a Ph.D. and Ed. S. in Special Education, Bilingual Education, and Language Reading and Culture from the University of Arizona. Her passion for protecting our environment as our Mother Earth (Pachamama) drives her to locate organizations or missions with the same goals to be of service to them as CAW Clergy.

Baby Witch Meets Dogma (and Doesn't Buy It) Smart Kid

By Doreen Lavista

'VE ALWAYS KNOWN I WAS A WITCH FROM THE very first make-believe magic in cartoons, to TV shows and movies. I knew I related to what was going on but…it wasn't really like that, all flash and make believe…real magic was subtle, organic. But I didn't know that yet.

Our family house was an Italian ranch, finished basement, main living space for Nana and Uncle John, upper level for Mommy Daddy, Debbie and me. It got cramped by the time I was three or four, so Mom had the attic finished into a bedroom.

The adults tried to put me to bed at a decent hour to get some grown-up time in. They could never talk freely around me…little ears, big mouth, and all that. So I went to bed and I guess I slept. But somewhere in the twilight of sleep, I left my body. I floated down the stairs and through the rooms, but I never touched the floor. It was as if I was the alien probe from "The Abyss." Down a second flight of stairs, I waited at the bannister rails and watched my family chit chat. I do not recall what they said, just that I floated there…and suddenly snapped back to the attic bedroom. I thought it was a dream, but it "felt so real." Didn't share it, and it never happened again.

My family was Italian Catholic, but both parents had been previously divorced. That made them excommunicated from the church. When they married, we, my sister and I were sent to parochial schools. Prior to their marriage, we would have not been accepted as students. The family celebrated the big holidays, but were not holy rollers, by any means.

We were required to attend Mass with our classmates on Sunday, but neither of my parents attended with us. So I never felt particularly compelled to continue to attend 9:00 Sunday Mass with the same kids I saw all week, when I could squeak into the 12:30 Mass with a couple of friends and get some pizza on the way home.

Picture it—Bronx NY 1966—I was seven years old, in first grade, wearing my plaid school uniform. We were preparing for our First Holy Communion and Sister Mary Roseanne was explaining the Holy Trinity to us. We. We already knew about God being the father of Jesus. But the dots did not all connect for me.

As Sister droned on about the Father, Son and Holy Ghost, the wheels in my head started turning.

My seven-year-old hand went up—"But, Sister.... If God the Father is Jesus' father...and He's GOD....doesn't that make Mary, as Jesus' Mother.... a GODDESS?"

And all forty-five little heads turned around and looked at me as if I were the fly in the ice cream. With perfect timing, Sister Mary Roseanne replied, "No, Doreen, Mary, a mortal woman is a saint, chosen by God for a special purpose[45], and she intercedes for us. That is, when we pray to her, she prays to God for us." Standard dogmatic programmed response.

Well, that didn't make any sense—why didn't God hear me without a third party? And what mortal woman could survive giving birth to a god—only a Goddess could do that. So, I got the vibe that it was better to comply, nod and smile than ask more questions (already a pariah) and I sat back down in my little wooden desk, mumbling to myself "you're not telling me the whole truth, I'll figure this out on my own." Kept my nose down until...puberty!

From then I completed twelve years of parochial schooling, received a wonderful education, but NEVER again bought into the whole Jesus thing. If they lied about that, what else did they lie about? The history would slowly unfold.

By age thirteen/fourteen (1973) I had found Anton LaVey, AE Waite, Crowley, Blavatsky, Leek and Gardner and did my own research on the burning times. I began reading Tarot at thirteen, studying from the witchcraft books of the time. There wasn't much to pick from on the bookstore and library shelves under "Occult", but the genre grew with me into the 70s and 80s.

Re-engaged the Goddess by fifteen—and again by twenty-six—I was having recurring dreams while pregnant and living in West Germany with my first husband. He would eventually abandon me,

---

[45]the older Me said, "special purpose, my ass."

but I never felt alone. She was always there. I prayed to Her and She answered. **That was the significant difference. I was heard.** My spells were working. She helped define my work. I dedicated to Her with Coven BellaDonna (New York and Connecticut) in the '90s. Raised my son Pagan.

Further associations led me to Salem MA, where I met Laurie Cabot, in Connecticut, Leo Martello and Janet Farrar, Byron Ballard in NC, and more recently Oberon Zell in Florida. I found my tribe

Although I support the theory of Mary Magdalene bearing the offspring of a Divine bloodline, I am not convinced that Jesus existed in the way the story has been presented. I see the parallels of prior mythologies attached to the Jesus story as the sacrificed god. Again, there's more to the story than they let on. What is presented to us as the teachings of Jesus have merit in healing the human condition, but I personally cannot seriously entertain organized Christianity or Roman Catholicism in its current incarnation.

I am currently an active eclectic Pagan priestess and practicing Witch with an established Reiki and Spiritual Wellness Coaching business in Crystal River, Florida.

Rev. Doreen Lavista, HPs, RMT is an Ordained Minister in the Universal Life Church, Reiki Master/Teacher, Intuitive Counselor and lifetime practitioner of Metaphysics with over 45 years' experience reading Tarot and engaging in Esoteric Healing Arts.

As an Affiliate Member of the International Center for Reiki training, she offers an earthy, common sense approach to spiritual well-being.

As a votary of the Divine Feminine, Doreen is committed to healing, empowerment, and transformation on a personal, local and planetary scale.

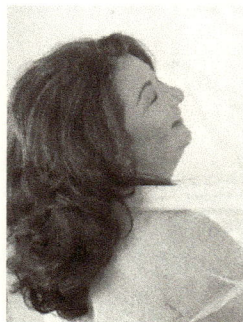

gone home to mother

By David Sterenchock (Minstrel Dave)

I was raised in the Ukrainian Catholic Church. I seldom participated in church activities. It was not pleasant and I did not enjoy it. Everything about it was too formal and repressive. There was also conflict because my Mother was not Catholic. I was forced to complete Communion classes, but after that my brothers, sister and I were pretty much left to our own devices.

I remember reading, "God created man in his own image." My first thought was, that's very sexist. Then I realized, Goddess created woman in her own image; thus the differences. Then I began seeing the Divinity inherent in the female.

I started frequenting a web site titled, "Spiritual Web Chat." In that chat I discovered many people with similar beliefs; however, there was quite the mix of theologies. It furthered my knowledge of and enabled me to see the Goddess potential in every woman who recognized and accepted the Goddessness in them.

Then I met my wife. We were friends in the aforementioned chat site for about seven or eight years. We shared similar beliefs. To meet and fall in love with someone with such similar beliefs is beyond what can be imagined. Seeing her as the Goddess incarnate made me realize she should always be treated as such.

My family does not really know how deep this goes and even if they did, they would have a hard time accepting it. Although my wife and I were wed/handfasted in a very ritualistic ceremony presided over by a Witch.

I had attended a few open circles and found the Pagan Community in that area to be very open and accepting. We made many friends within that community. After moving away from Pennsylvania and relocating to Idaho we have been mostly a Coven of two.

I am now firmly established as a Goddess worshipper even though my Divine wife has recently gone home to Mother. However, this has not changed my belief system in any way. Once a

Goddess, always a Goddess.

Currently, I write songs, many of which are Pagan. I do solitary rituals since losing the Love of my Life and I maintain a Facebook page started by my wife. I try to retain her sense of openness and convey useful information. I also play music at Renaissance Faires and hope to resume that aspect of my life when I relocate back East.

As for Jesus. I do believe he was a prophet and a teacher but his work has been subverted by his followers and their church.

I would tell anyone of any religion this: "One man's myth is another man's religion. Tolerance is key in living in a kaleidoscopic world."

Minstrel Dave, Born March 20, 1954 and too old to know any better.

when the goddess calls

By Kate Dennis

IKE A LOT OF KIDS IN MY GENERATION, I was brought up pseudo-Christian: the kids were trucked off to church while the parents stayed home. In my case it was the Roman Catholic Church, although I did occasionally visit other denominations. Looking back, none of them ever felt quite right, so as soon as I headed to college I stopped attending organized church.

I missed the fellowship and intellectual stimulation of a spiritual gathering place, so for a while I experimented with meditation groups and Buddhism, attended meetings and workshops sponsored by several fringe religions. I even explored witchcraft briefly. None of them kept my interest for any length of time…except witchcraft.

A friend who was an Episcopalian invited me to a service at his parish…and to my surprise…I loved it. So much so that I kept going back until I became an Episcopalian in my early 20s. My Catholic family, who only attended church on Christmas, Easter, funerals, weddings and baptisms, were beside themselves: "at least she didn't become a witch!" Little did they know.

I loved the Episcopal Church so much that I practically lived in the building of the local parish. I joined every guild and group available, eventually becoming a Lay Minister. I loved the sound of the sung liturgy, the music, the processions; it was magical and transported me to another realm of reality. I never missed a service. The diocesan Bishop took notice of my dedication and pulled me in for a talk about becoming a fully-ordained minister under Can, a church law that allowed ordination prior to attending seminary. I eagerly agreed, and after ordination became a chaplain directly assigned to his office. This gave me the freedom to minister in any role and assignment. I worked in a variety of ministries – hospitals, prisons, as an interim rector to parishes, and as a representative with the local interfaith group for nearly 25 years. And I loved it, good and bad. Jesus and I were tight, although I held a special affection for Mary, his mother.

It was Mary whom I consulted and prayed to in the times I sought divine intervention and advice. Within my individual spiritual development I'd joined a women's group who met to share their faith traditions through meditation, chanting, drumming and deep discussion. Fully half of them were from Earth-centered traditions...and some were witches.

I had been drawn to Wicca in college and attended workshops with Judy Harrow and Marion Weinstein and in my spare time frequented the infamous Magickal Childe bookstore. I was attracted to the wonder and strangeness of the occult in my teen years, and now I was acting on it. I never stopped reading and learning about the Craft even while attending seminary. The two just paralleled one another for me. I studied ancient religions and gods while my classmates earned degrees in Bible Studies. In the end my own post graduate degree became Comparative Religion. Unknowingly, I was preparing myself to become a Pagan.

I had an understanding early on that Mary was considered to be a form of the Great Goddess, and the knowledge of that chipped away at me until I understood I could no longer be a Christian. In studying for my degree I gathered as much information on NeoPaganism, folk medicine, lore and magick as I could I examined occult traditions-no easy task at that time because most traditions were still very secretive and books were few. My personal exploration was eclectic: I attended lectures and workshops with Michael Harner and Sandra Ingerman, Chief Oren Lyons, Judy Harrow and others. The words of all these teachers blended into my own tradition. The Truth I learned through exposure to all this information was that Gaia, the Great Mother, and the archetypes of gods and goddesses formed the Divine.I refuse to pick at scabs with Christian friends, those who are clergy in particular. They know the failures and pitfalls of Christianity as well as I. They are aware of the trauma and damage done through greed and the love of power. They know right from wrong...and so do I. With as much issue as I have with Christianity as an organization, I still consider Jesus as a great prophet whose words have benefit for humankind. The essence of his teachings ring true in too many situations for me to deny their value.

89

Through these years my experience with the Pagan community has been mixed. Even though I've encountered some who treat me suspiciously because of my former affiliation with Christianity (I understand why) things have landed on a positive note. It is difficult to argue the fine points, even though I welcome healthy discussion. Frankly, I no longer try because I am confident in my belief. I know what's right for me may not be right for others. So mote it be. Those in the community have been gracious hosts, lively conversationalists, wonderful teachers and lifelong companions. I am grateful for what I consider to be an authentic relationship with the Great Mother, for I can bring anything to her and know I will not be shamed or made to feel less. It is a beauty and wholeness I cannot describe but feel with my whole being.

May we be blessed in Her Name!

Kate Dennis (1956) has been writing the blog AmethJera's Broom with A View for over a decade. She serves the larger community through spiritual direction and as a priestess dedicated to Bridget of Ireland, and holds PhDs in Comparative Religion and Forensic Psychology. She currently lives quietly with her cat Charlie in the heart of rural Appalachia.

I am not a preacher, I am a pagan

By Aelwyn Telcontar (Rev. Luis A. Valadez)

I WAS BORN TO A FAMILY OF MIXED RELIGIOUS background. My mother was involved in Santeria and was an active Santera. My stepfather, who entered the picture when I was around 4, was a Mexican-American child of the 1970s involved in smoking pot and New Age concepts and who hated organized religion. On top of Santeria, my mother was also a member of the National Organization of Women (NOW) and dabbled in Goddess spirituality.

Being Mexican-American, and my mother being more religious than my father, we did the only thing Hispanics do: attend the Catholic Church. I attended faithfully, completed CCD religious education classes and was subsequently confirmed with St. Francis of Assisi as my patron. At the same time I studied mythology, the occult and paranormal activity well into my preteens.

I didn't grow up in an idyllic setting. I won't go into too much detail except to say that I was exposed to sex at a very early age, and was molested and abused for a number of years. It wasn't a member of the family but someone in the neighborhood. Add to this that I had liked boys since I was five and was struggling with my sexual identity. I was a very warped and confused boy, hearing messages about masculinity while also being teased at school for being too "girly." My only escape was the world of books, which still provides an escape for me when things get stressful.

I have an older adopted sister who converted to Pentecostal Christianity when I was about twelve or thirteen. She moved in with us and my mother warned me about her "possible cult that she attends." One night I knocked on her door and she welcomed me in. She was nice and sweet which wasn't the norm. She had been hooligan but found a genuine change of heart with her conversion to "Born-Again Christianity." She sat there and read the Bible opened up to the Book of Revelation and began expounding to me on the rewards of heaven. I didn't hear anything she was telling me, except one phrase that stood out: "If you accept Jesus Christ into your heart, you will be a new person. Any struggles with sin God will take away." That's it—I was hooked! I envisioned all of the unwelcome thoughts and feelings of liking boys, the uncomfortable sexual liaisons that left me scarred in many emotional and mental ways, the constant feeling of being unwelcome and unwanted because of being too "girly." Who was I to resist such a tempting offer?

I said the "Prayer of Salvation" and then began to repeat the word "Hallelujah" as a mantra. Within seconds, I felt a rush of energy through me, flowing in and around me. I felt a powerful wave encompass me, and my lips and tongue began to move of their own accord. I had been "baptized in the Spirit," or "filled with the Holy Ghost." I was now a born-again, Spirit-filled Christian on my way to heaven! My older adopted sister didn't think it was right at the time for me to announce my conversion to my mom, but I did the opposite. It was 11pm, and my mom happened to come out of the room to get a drink of water. I told her that I had been "saved," and she told me, "Luis, I'm tired. But please be careful with what Melinda tells you, ok?" She turned and went back to bed.

The next day I woke up feeling like a new person. In quick succession I purchased a Bible (New International Version), and took my first trip to the church my older adopted sister attended. Jesus Ministries, Inc. was an African-American Pentecostal Holiness Church that had schismed from its parent organization, the Church of the Living God, the Pillar and Ground of Truth (extracted from 1 Timothy 3:15). The mother organization had been founded by woman evangelist named Mary Magdalena L. Tate in 1903, and is still one of the oldest African-American churches in existence today. The church service at Jesus Ministries was spontaneous with preaching, healing by laying-on-of-hands, choir praise and worship, and intense teaching. Everyone showed up with their Bibles, pens and notebooks; the good Reverend taught everyone to study, take notes and memorize Scripture. Having the background of a voracious reader, I quickly read through the Bible and memorized as much as I could.

But as much as I found a new faith, there were some things I couldn't shake. I remembered my dad's lessons to me when I was younger comparing the different versions of the Bible. There were footnotes in my NIV Bible not present in other people's King James

Bible, footnotes such as "This Scripture is not found in original documents," or "These verses were added later on and are not found in original manuscripts." I didn't voice my concerns, only observed. I was too afraid to say anything. Besides, coming from a Hispanic and Catholic background, you never questioned authority. Ever. The Pastor and the Elders were wiser than I was, so I listened and took notes with everyone else. But there were still things I didn't understand, like why didn't my homosexual feelings go away like God promised? Why was learning about extraterrestrial life so hell-worthy? Why was everyone going to hell except us? Why do I lose my salvation if I *think* thoughts? I didn't realize God was so ultra-strict—no wonder we had 4 services a week! The average Sunday service was about 5-7 hours long, depending if we had fasted or not.

I had gone from one abusive environment to another, only this time it was in the form of religion. But I didn't recognize it at that time. I just sat and listened.

Just when I was having my doubts about this new religion:
BAM!

Our church hosted two evangelists from two different places, one from Cocoa Beach, and the other from Trinidad and Tobago. Both preached on different nights, and I almost didn't make the first service because of work. I was a skinny little nobody who was trying to do good when all of a sudden I had a prophecy exclaimed over me from the first preacher (a female prophetess). She announced to the Church that I had a great destiny in my life and that I was meant to be a televangelist. She laid hands on me and said that God would use me for His purposes. I dropped down because of the intense energy. Two days later the second evangelist (a male apostle I learned) also called me out and said that I was anointed from my mother's womb. I had a great destiny and that I would preach to the world, I would be on television and I had been singled out from my entire family for this great purpose. Again, hands laid on, and passed out "under the power."

Now please allow me to explain something. Pentecostal Christians believe that the same prophecies and healings which were active during the Time of Jesus are also active in the world today. Pentecostals are concerned with reviving the practices and offices of the Early Apostolic Church; in essence, there are modern-day apostles, prophets and healers. So when two different people from two different places proclaim a shared prophecy over you on two separate days, it's taken seriously. Thus began everyone watching me and keeping an eye on me for future ministries. That was it—my fate had been set and written in stone. My childhood dream of wanting to be a paleontologist was out the window, and instead I would now be a minister to the world. Quiet, shy little me who was always teased and abused, would become a televangelist. I was 14.

A year later, I began to preach and teach. I began to be involved with other ministries within the church. I dove headlong into community service and volunteering. My entire family, save for my father, had now converted and began attending the church: my grandmother, my older adopted sister, myself, and my younger brother and sister. In addition, not only was my family celebrating together but I found that trying to be good and stay busy "being about the Lord's work" would hopefully recompense for all of the nasty sex thoughts that invaded my teen life.

I hated myself, and I hated what I was doing in my bedroom. Solitary enjoyment was "the devil's claws on your parts, making them burn with sin." We weren't just Pentecostal, we were Pentecostal Holiness. That meant staying pure and living a God-filled life, lest your salvation be taken away from you. No secular music, no drinking, no sports, no movies, no dating, no sex, no profanity. Not even the news or newspapers. No Disney. Nothing. My mother took many things from our childhood including video games, movies and books and burned (yes, burned) them all. Burning books and ungodly paraphernalia was the only sure way to "break Satan's curse over the house" so my father could be saved—poor fellow. We began to have prayer meetings and Bible studies at my home. I taught more, and was eventually welcomed as a Minister in the church.

But then the nightmare began...

When I was 16, I was raped in broad daylight by a customer who "liked" me. The following night at a service I told one of the deacons what happened, and she in turn told one of the ministers. He threatened me with telling my mother if I didn't tell her. Alone, hurt and confused I told my mom what happened after we arrived home from service. My mother had to leave the room because she didn't want to beat me for "not being a man" and losing the rape battle. A few days later I was forced to recount in front of my Pastor, his wife, and my mom the details of the rape. The Pastor then proceeded to say that it must have been something in me that attracted that man to me. "After all," he said, "If God was really with you, why didn't He tell you not to go that way? What did you do to block communion with God?" He performed an exorcism to rid me of the suspected "homosexual demon," and the next Sunday I was preached about as an example of how you think your heart is a pure diamond, "but there is a tiny speck of homosexuality that can block your communion with God." I was embarrassed and ashamed.

Committing suicide was a sure way to hell, and I couldn't rebel and leave the church. So I figured I was in the wrong, and once again everyone else was right. I tried to move past everything, and eventually earned enough trust from my Pastor in a year to become a Minister. I was also accepted by Oral Roberts University, which I attended for a while. I didn't graduate, however, because we didn't have money. I ended up coming back and preparing for God's Ministry at home. We re-opened up prayer meetings and Bible studies. I started having more friends come to the church and join, proof that I was a real evangelist. I underwent ministerial training through Global Ministries Resource Network (GMRN), a groundbreaking ministry designed to lead and teach future apostles and prophets. The minister from Trinidad returned and proclaimed that I had a prophetic calling and as a result, I joined the GMRN School of Prophets. Soon, I was handpicked by the head Apostle of GMRN for one-on-one training. He heard of the prophecies over me, and figured that I was an "apostle-in-training."

A few years later I found myself as an Assistant Minister to an apostle and pastor in Sunrise, Florida. By now I had left the original church I grew up in. I had a 15-minute radio program called, "Did You Know?" and taught their Seminary program. I preached and taught services, and was a licensed and ordained minister. The ministry was known nationally and even on television. They were preparing to break ground on their newly purchased 5 acres of land for their new church that would launch televised services. I was going to be a part of it. At last...was the prophecy coming true?

Throughout all of this adventure, I was also exploring New Age concepts on the side. Why? Well, I'm curious. That's always been a part of me, wanting to learn more and more. Part of that is because of what my father taught me, to open my mind, expand my horizons, and lead a fulfilling life. Part of it, however, was also due to the contradictions that I was seeing. I began to read the Bible in Hebrew and Greek. I began to study Church History: schisms, political intrigue, genocide of indigenous populations, and slavery. I began to talk with Jewish rabbis and ask them why they didn't believe in Jesus. After all, it was plain to us Christians why Jesus IS the Messiah—how could the Jews be so stubborn? A very kindly rabbi with sneakers (who was about 80) was patient enough with me to answer my questions, and show me the differences in translation and understanding with Hebrew prophecies. I found out about televangelist scandals involving money, prostitutes, and drugs. I began to realize that I would have become one of those people. It was a nightmare that I wrestled with for many, many years. No televangelist was free from scandal, and that included my apostle/pastor who was in the newspaper a few months after I left his church for financial mismanagement.

While studying Judaism and science (because Creationism was no longer making sense), I also began to read about alternative religions including Witchcraft and Paganism. I was still preaching and teaching, but I began to have doubts about what I was doing. I began to lose faith in Christianity, and in myself. I realized I was living someone else's life. I was living someone else's dictum. I had never dealt with the abuse in my childhood, the ordeal after my rape or my sexual orientation. I was still depending on authority figures to do things for me, to carry me to greatness; a greatness that was packed with misinformation. On a heartbreaking day in August 2004, I finally broke away from it all. I was tired of living my gay lifestyle in secret and not truly discovering who I was. I was done. I left the Church and the same day was hired at a local McDonald's for minimum wage, a place where no one knew who I was or where I came from. I was determined to make my own life and write my own destiny.

Today I am co-pastor at a public Pagan Temple in Palm Bay, Florida. I am also the Hierophant and Kurios for the Ophic Strix Tradition, a Hellenic Witchcraft Mystery Tradition. I have been involved with open circles, Wizardry, Druidry and Wicca. I have been with Strega witches and studied with the Sufis at the local mosque. I have contributed articles to Witchvox [the Witches Voice website] and am now here, writing this for you all to know where I came from. My quest to learn from other faiths has never gone away, and instead I proudly embrace the word "Pagan."

Paganism has taught me so much, and I have learned a lot from people such as Oberon Zell-Ravenheart, Tony Mierzwicki, Raven Grimmasi, Philip Carr-Gomm, John Michael Greer and others. I correspond with Witches famous and not. I love my faith, and most of all I have forgiven Christianity and the people from my past. I have also forgiven myself.

My fellowship in the Order of Bards, Ovates and Druids taught me to respect Christians and really gave me a Pagan "Malcolm X" moment when I was corrected of the idea that all Christians were evil and responsible for the so-called Burning Times. My bitterness towards the failure of Christianity was not in the faith itself, but in the people. Personality cults were the root of my faith, and that was a difficult concept to accept. In spite of it all, I remained with Paganism because even when I studied "Esoteric Christianity;" its echoes were that of Pagan Cosmologies and Myths. What I practice today is not ancient, but it is fulfilling. It has taken so long to understand the basic tenets of Paganism—personal responsibility, love of wisdom, interconnectedness, sacred ecology, etc.—are what I needed. I needed to make my own way, to weave my own Fate and learn to take actions for myself.

The long, hard road was worth it. My mother and older adopted sister are still Christian. My father and my siblings have embraced Paganism. So has my husband. Our religion is a family affair, one in which I am proud to lead. I am in medical school, with the aim of being a health care provider one day. I am going back to school with the love and support of my family. I am not a preacher, I am a Pagan, following in the footsteps of my ancestors. I feel like the spiritual practices of my faith have given me a profound sense of my place in the world. Unlike Christianity where I was a star-in-the-making, Paganism gives me the reality check: I am a speck of star stuff in a vast Cosmos. I am comfortable with that, because you know what? I am home.

communing with the goddess

By Michael Starsheen

I GREW UP IN A CHRISTIAN SCIENTIST HOUSE-hold. We were devout, but realistic. If we had an injury or a broken bone it was cared for properly by the medical community, but we didn't get vaccinated or otherwise do most of the medical things that most people do. We went to church every Sunday, starting at the First Church of Christ, Scientist in Birmingham, Alabama. We moved to Mobile, Alabama, and eventually to San Francisco, California in 1965, where we attended the Ninth Church of Christ, Scientist. I actively attended Sunday school, and learned lessons from the Bible and from the *Science and Health with Key to the Scriptures* by Mary Baker Eddy.

While in Birmingham, I was unable to attend first grade due to legal cutoff dates over birthdays in October, so my parents enrolled me in a religious school with the All Saints Episcopal Church. They required religious training as part of the school curriculum, so I was exposed to more mainstream Christian religious concepts for a year. But I didn't get real religious education in mainstream Christianity until my parents divorced in 1969.

My mother moved us back to Birmingham from San Francisco, and due to my father's well-known presence in the Christian Science church there, she decided to convert to being a Methodist like her elder sister. We attended the Trinity United Methodist Church in Homewood, Alabama. That was when I was baptized and started religious education. I was 12 years old, and at the age where I noticed how different the beliefs were in Methodism than in Christian Science, as well as the behavior of people in the church. I attended Sunday school, youth meetings on Sunday evenings, and the occasional revival.

It bothered me a great deal that the Methodists preached against liquor and smoking, yet the first thing many people did as soon as they exited the church on Sunday was to light up. My mother served wine to her bridge club members, and I saw other people drinking wine and spirits at different times. Add to that my first reaction to communion, where I'd been told the cups had wine and I instantly knew it was Welch's grape juice instead. (Welch's was originally made as a substitute communion drink for the Methodists.) These things bothered me a lot. I tended to question everything because it didn't make sense to me, given my previous religious experiences.

So, when I went to college at a Methodist school, I didn't continue to attend services. It didn't have the meaning to me that it did to my family because I saw too much contradiction between the teachings and the hypocrisy of the people who "believed." I joined the Society for Creative Anachronism, where met my first Wiccan teachers. I found the beliefs of the God and the Goddess to be much more palatable than Christianity, and the believers were more morally inclined to follow the teachings of "an ye harm none, do as ye will." I began studying astrology and the Tarot despite my training in physics and mathematics at the school, mostly because what the teachers were saying about those subjects struck me as opinions they'd been given but not based on actual experience. I felt like I had come home to a place I could believe in.

Then, I met my husband, who insisted I give up "all the woo-woo stuff" if we were going to stay together because he couldn't deal with it. Idiotically, I did so, and joined a local Lutheran church in Cocoa, Florida. That lasted for several years, but eventually we both drifted away from the church because it didn't satisfy our beliefs. I became an atheist for a time.

Eventually, the abuse I suffered from my husband drove me into disability, and I went back into my studies of Wicca and the gods, and my work with astrology and the Tarot. I learned mostly from books, primarily Scott Cunningham's *Wicca for the Solitary Practitioner*, and D. J. Conway's *Celtic Magic*. I was trying to learn to work with the gods of my Celtic heritage, and developed a comfortable practice. Then I met Deborah Nix and joined the Fellowship of Isis.

I did also take time to meditate in nature and allow myself to open to hearing the gods' words. I had several visions, and began studying for the priesthood. One evening, I went out on my porch to meditate with the Moon, which was conjunct Venus in the sky. I saw a face form below the Moon's crescent, which was on her head. The light of Venus shone nearby as part of her staff. I stood entranced for a long time, communing with the Goddess, until she indicated that she felt I was worthy of working with her.

I did not know who had summoned me at the time, but through meditation and study, I realized that it was Isis. My first reaction was, "Not the Egyptians, that's too weird," but eventually I settled down and accepted I'd been called to a path I was unprepared to follow. Through the Fellowship of Isis, I began to study Egyptian mythology and magic more deeply.

I had other visions during my training: Bast and Nuit of Egypt called me to their service;, Bast for creativity and Nuit for wisdom. I received a vision of Odin, who also called me to his service. Ultimately, I was ordained a priestess of Isis, Bast, and Nuit in October of 1994.

In an FOI ritual called Eros and Psyche that the local FOI group performed with a group from Pensacola, Florida, I drew down and manifested the goddess Juno of Rome. Hera, Juno's Greek counterpart, called to me strongly, and helped me escape my abusive relationship and begin to stand on my own. I owe her a great debt.

I studied for the Hierophancy in the Fellowship, which is a service that works with the liturgy and teaches people to become priests and priestesses. I became a hierophant in October of 1995. I communicated a great deal by mail with Lady Olivia Robertson, one of the founders of the Fellowship, and created a web page for people to join. She appointed me as an Archpriestess in the Fellowship in 1996. I continued serving the Goddess in Sunnyvale, California, where I had moved to get free of my marriage completely.

When I began going to their convocations in 1998, I met many people through Isis Oasis and the Fellowship and ultimately became an Archdruid in the Druid Clan of Dana and a Knight Commander in the Noble Order of Tara in the 2000s. (These are both environmentally aligned service organizations within the FOI.) I studied alchemy with Deena Butta of the Chicago FOI, and became a Solar Alchemist in 2007 after writing *Universal Alchemy* as a study piece.

I was also inspired to write a book about Greek mythology in 2006, where I channeled each of the Greek gods and goddesses to tell their sides of their stories. The result was my book, *Mythic Voices*. I've written a number of other books and study guides since that time, all self-published through Lulu.

I also went through a personal transformation that profoundly affected my relationship with the gods: I transitioned from female to male, and became legally Michael Starsheen in 2008. I began to work more towards a balance of god and goddess energies in my spiritual practices, which continue to this day. I teach for the Fellowship of Isis, and have a temple complex at my home in Dunsmuir, California, where I serve the gods on a daily basis.

I still believe in Jesus and his teachings, as they provide a good moral foundation for life in the world; however, I reject the teachings of Peter and Paul on which most of Christian religion is founded as they are too exclusionary. I also reject the church's attitudes toward Paganism, which I find repugnant. I am a member of the Unitarian Universalist church in San Jose, California, but as I no longer live there, I am inactive.

For other Christians and those who still believe, I'm glad that they are comfortable in their beliefs, if it serves them. If it doesn't, if they begin to question some of the strictures of the Church, such as those surrounding the subordination of women, I suggest that they look to the Goddess to learn a more balanced way of belief.

The Right Reverend Michael Starsheen is an Archpriest Hierophant of the Fellowship of Isis, and operates the Temple of Isis of the Stars as part of New Karnak Center in Dunsmuir, California. He is an archdruid, knight commander, and solar alchemist in the Fellowship as well, services to the Gods he has been called to follow. He is the author of a number of self-published books, including Mythic Voices *and* Universal Alchemy. *He is also an artist and does illustrations for his books.*

out the door

By Mary Alice Wittnebert

I WAS BORN IN 1954 AS AN ONLY CHILD. I SAW very early that my mother and father didn't get along. As soon as I learned to say the word "no," my mother started trying to bring me into line with her own controlled and overly strict upbringing. She was hypercritical and usually angry. I felt unloved and lonely.

All my life I was interested in that which can't be perceived with the five senses.

I was absorbed in books all my childhood and was drawn to stories about fairies, witches, magic. Some of my favorites were *The Witch of Blackbird Pond* (actually in part about intolerance), *An Enemy at Green Knowe, Hubble's Bubble* (both definitely magical), the Mrs. Piggle Wiggle books (she wasn't a witch but she had magical powers) and the Prydain series by Lloyd Alexander. I'm sure I wished I could wave a wand and change everything: make my parents happy, "win friends and influence people." But the fact is, I was drawn to things I now understand have to do with the Craft.

I loved mythology and found it much more interesting than church/ Sunday school – regardless of the country of origin, I loved the idea of a multitude of deities.

I liked ghost stories especially when supposedly true (though ideally not scary). I loved the idea of ghosts/spirits remaining in an old place. I loved and felt connected to old and historical places and that love only strengthened over time.

I liked the idea of witches—I was scared of the stereotypical ugly and malicious old woman, but intrigued by the idea of a beautiful and powerful witch (hopefully benevolent like Glinda, but I liked Maleficent!). My best friend and I pretended to be witches and invented "Spookland," a small patch of woods next to the local brook. We went there every chance we got and pretended to do magic.

The desire to find out more about this world was quashed partly by my parents, partly by education, and a lot by the church later. As a child, you're told, "There's no such thing as a ghost!" "There's no such thing as a witch!" I was disappointed. Little did I know!

I loved stones and precious metals from a very young age; we had jewelers' catalogues, so all my fantasies were about the cardinal stones! But I got interested in geology, had a rock collection, picked up all sorts of interesting rocks outdoors, and then, in line with an increasing interest in the theory of universal energy, I got curious about the idea that stones have energies/powers.

My parents were not religious, so I escaped the dominating influence on friends who were raised, say, Catholic. Church meant nothing to Daddy; he attended major holidays out of conformity. He loved nature; he had such strong ties to it, it's as if that was his church. I went with him to the woods and remembered what he taught me. He also loved gardening.

So I grew up with a connection to nature, which, combined with reading mythology, started a connection between nature and deity. Daddy wouldn't have bought into that; he was extremely logical, and distrustful of unscientific thinking, and of anything affected by emotion rather than by common sense. However, he had a copy of *The White Goddess*. I tried to read it and thought Graves was all over the place, never finished it, ended up giving it away, but I wondered why in the world Daddy read it. I assumed just out of intellectual curiosity. Religion was foreign to him; once when we talked about it he said he was more or less a Deist, so he had concluded that there was a creator spirit. I wonder what he thought of the Goddess and of the theory of a Goddess-centered culture that had been overtaken by monotheism. I wonder if that struck a chord with him somewhere.

Mommy was raised Presbyterian but disliked its strictness and rigidity. She became an Episcopalian, attending church every Sunday. But neither of my parents were conventional Christians. Both had some concept of "God," but I don't think even Mommy was 100% vested in the idea of the Savior, and Daddy very definitely did not believe any of it. Daddy viewed the Bible as an interesting but suspect collection of ancient documents, and Mommy struggled, I believe, trying to practice the Beatitudes and frustrated when she failed. In my family I never heard one word against any other religion, or any other race. The main thing Daddy rebuked me for was

making generalizations. As far as he was concerned, any idea beginning with "they" had a hole in it.

The Episcopal doctrine I was exposed to was broadminded; the
Church later became one of the first to ordain women and gays. The
problems I had with amusements and sexual activity stemmed from
Mommy, who had a lot of issues. In retrospect I feel sorry for her
because she bet on having a kid she could raise exactly as she was
raised in a society exactly like the one she knew since her birth in
1919. Instead ,she got rock and roll, beatniks, sex, drugs, hippies and
protesters and she hated every second.

From the time I first read *The Sound of Music* in the 1960s,
where she wrote that in Maria von Trapp's convent they were taught
that the most important thing in life is "to find out the will of God
and to do it", I agreed—but in the context of finding out what you
are supposed to do in your life with or without religion. You are
created for a specific purpose and it is vital to find out what that is
in order to be at your best in your life.

Because I was unhappy growing up in a contentious household,
the Jesus movement attracted me; I was looking for loving kindness,
and someplace to belong. A friend invited me to an independent
Pentecostal church, where I sat through the whole thing and cried
bitterly, longing to believe and unable to do so.

The pastor issued an altar call at the end of the service. My boyfriend went to the altar and said "Come on!" so I went. That was
1972, the beginning of decades of fits and starts, in and out of
churches, trying to believe and not fully able to drink the Kool-Aid.
I never could believe 100% no matter how hard I tried—even when
I thought it was "true". I read almost the entire Bible—always ex-
cepting Numbers and Deuteronomy! —so I could see why some
people said it contradicted itself.

Jesus said the two greatest commandments were to love God and
love your neighbor, and "on these two commandments hang all the
Law and the Prophets," so I clung to that simple teaching But a lot
of my coreligionists didn't, which stuck in my craw. And oh, how
terrified I was that I was going to hell myself, as well as my *entire
family* – they, because they didn't believe, and I, because if I sinned
or backslid and Jesus returned at that moment, I would be left behind.

I never could figure out what my purpose was, or what God's
will was. At 50, I realized I wanted to see things as they really are,

not as I thought they ought to be and not as I wished they were. I stopped going to church and did some very hard thinking for two years. I had a tough decision to make regarding my marriage. When I decided I had to get out, it was the first time in my life I had reasoned my way to a sensible conclusion; all the rest of the time I had been running on my emotions and "received wisdom" about Jesus and the Bible. It opened the door for a complete change in approach, one not involving "God's will."

I left my husband in 2005 and became involved with a wonderful man whose bookshelf was full of Pagan literature—*The Solitary Witch, Wicca for the Solitary Practitioner*, and Blum's *Book of Runes*, among others. Phil had been raised Catholic and walked out. He was more of a theoretical pagan than a practicing one—he used to say he didn't believe if you lit a green candle and said a bunch of things you'd get money—but he believed in Nature and polytheism. Being with him sparked my latent Paganism and brought to fruition all the influences and attractions of my childhood.

While with Phil, I reasoned my way out of Christianity. If in fact there was a Creator—I hadn't moved on to the Goddess yet—who had made everything and everybody, what "father" worth his salt condemns his kids to hellfire? I do believe in a created universe, but I rejected the concept of hell, and if there's no hell, there's no need for salvation or for a savior. I then found a book called *The Case for God*, by Karen Armstrong. Armstrong traced the development of Judaism from the Far East, as it migrated west; she traced the exact path of all the books of the Bible, what was happening when they were formulated, and how circumstances influenced them. She traced the founding of Christianity and of Islam. Her scholarly, chapter-and-verse exposition was the Maxwell's Silver Hammer to what was left of my Christianity, confirming the vague 1 ideas I picked up from my parents. Christianity ended up being a veneer that wore off of what I really believed and was drawn to.

Now I run from anything to do with Christianity; it's like I fear that it'll reach out and strangle me. I don't disrespect Jesus but the only thing I'm comfortable with is what I remember of his teachings about love and compassion. I know exactly what my former church friends would say about the path I've chosen and I will not expose myself to them. I recognize that I'm antagonistic, and that antagonism indicates something I need to heal. All my life I hated being bossed around in any way, yet, being an insecure teenager when I became "born again," I believed it when they told me I was going to hell if I didn't "accept Jesus," and I struggled with that fear for over 40 years. I won't risk having that fear reawakened if it's only sleeping and not dead.

Phil died of a massive heart attack in 2011. I was ready to curl up and die. Before I made my choice to end my marriage, I had had to acknowledge the death of the fantasy of "happily ever after" and it broke my heart. Phil's death just put the lid on it. I didn't care if I got hit by a semi.

Yet there were so many serendipities—a friend who pointed me toward Buddhist ideas and thinking, my first tarot reading, meeting and befriending genuine psychics, mediums and Witches, who always had an energy I was drawn to and who always welcomed me. My mother's caregivers from 2007-2011 were Christian women from Guyana whose spirituality combined Anglicanism with African and Indian beliefs and practices, integrating them effortlessly, and enabling them to counsel me about spiritual matters and comfort me when Phil died. All these people, Witches or not, were thinkers outside the box.

In 2016 I moved to eastern Pennsylvania and immediately visited Shooting for the Moon, a Wiccan shop and spiritual center. I asked how to find out more. They said, start coming to rituals. My first one was Full Moon in October 2016. I started taking classes in January 2017, and I've learned more spiritually and emotionally since then, than I did in my entire life—far more than when I was in the church. I progressed to where I wanted to see what was going to happen to me rather than wishing I'd never been born. When I was interviewed before starting classes, they asked me what I wanted and I didn't even have to think about it: I said "I want the truth!" Thus my chosen ritual name, Verity, came to me naturally.

Shooting for the Moon's focus is eclectic, Celtic and Gardnerian, so our pantheon is Celtic with the Goddess is paramount. My not having a good relationship with my mother has worked in my favor regarding Her. If I'd had a positive mother figure I might not have been attracted to the idea of a Goddess as nurturer and teacher, because I wouldn't have felt the lack. I don't call Her by any particular name; She is just there, each and all. In my mind She is most like Pomona, because of my love for nature and gardening.

The current membership of Shooting for the Moon is six of us who have completed First Degree, a seventh taking class, and the

Temple's founder. Any of us can serve as high priest or priestess in a ritual. I love it whether I'm leading or participating. When I serve as priestess there are moments when the words come out of my mouth that I don't remember much about it afterwards; I feel like I channeled Her at those times. When I do a ritual at home, it's usually on behalf of somebody else and I don't write the words, but the same thing happens—it pours out of me and then I don't remember much

Very few people outside of the Craft know that I practice, but between my tattoos, boho clothes and jewelry and my energy, fellow believers often recognize me! I don't discuss it with anybody but them, because my journey is mine. I follow a lot of pagan Facebook pages and benefit from what is shared there, as well as sharing my own experiences for their benefit.

The only thing I can say to Christians who are starting to question whether there is more than what they've heard, is that there IS more – more to find out, more to do, more to be. As there is always light from the Sun and Moon, so there are infinite paths of light toward the Goddess.

Mary Alice Wittnebert is semi-retired and lives in Catasauqua, Pennsylvania in a converted 19th-century storefront apartment, with three cats and hundreds of books. She loves making art, landscape photography, and genealogy.

from churchgoing christian to solitary pagan

By Steve Provost

AFTER RECEIVING A VERY CORDIAL E-mail from a Christian friend of mine, I was spurred to write down some of the steps in my spiritual journey from churchgoing Christian to (mostly) solitary Pagan. I thought my Christian friends—and a few others—might wonder why I embarked on this journey, so I decided to share my thoughts with them

I spent about 15 years in the evangelical church, and I don't regret the time spent there. I learned many things that contributed greatly to my spiritual understanding and critical thinking ability. I didn't leave because I felt I was somehow mistreated there; I don't have a sob story or an ax to grind. I left for ethical reasons.

I was disturbed by some of behavior that "the church" engaged in because it seemed coercive and manipulative. I did a great deal of study, in part because I sought, at one point, to write a biography of Jesus. But in the course of this study, I saw numerous internal inconsistencies in the Bible—and, more troubling, inconsistencies between the passages "the church" was citing and the principles Jesus espoused. I became convinced that this organized religious structure called "the church" seemed to be doing many of the same things that the Pharisees in Jesus' day were doing.

He called them "whitewashed tombs"—clean and appealing on the outside, filthy on the inside—and indicted them for being hypocrites. At the end of the day, I felt that I could either stay in "the church" and compromise ethics I considered to be consistent with Jesus' teachings or violate my understanding of those teachings and choose to leave. My ultimate decision was to leave, just as Jesus had ventured outside the orthodox religious structure of his day. He was demonized for healing or picking heads of grain on the Sabbath, when no one listened to his explanation that the Sabbath was made for man, not vice versa. He tried to reform it and was crucified for the attempt. If the cleansing of the temple was an act of sheer frustration at others' unwillingness to listen, I could understand it. I experienced the same frustration myself in the evangelical church.

You may think I'm equating myself to Jesus, but I am not. He was light years ahead of me in the humility department and in his understanding of the human psyche. What I see today in "the church" is a pompous arrogance and an insecurity that bears itself out in an insatiable desire to "be right." When I identified myself as a Christian, I never understood how the followers of an all-powerful creator could possibly be so insecure as to be scared of the devil. That struck me as a dualistic idea inconsistent with the Judeo-Christian tradition that Yahweh created all things. And insecurity, I have learned, is the opposite of humility.

Jesus was nothing if not humble and secure in himself. Despite great pressure to the contrary, he told his followers to lay down their swords and pray in private. To me, these courageous actions didn't square too well with those of the modern church which seems intent on forcing its ideas off on others to reinforce its own fragile, egotistical belief that it has cornered the market on truth.

I am referring to "the church" here intentionally. I once posted a cartoon on my Facebook page that said, "Jesus, save me from your followers." However, after doing so I regretted it because it lumped all Christians together into the same category. That was insensitive and inaccurate, and to those who saw that cartoon, I apologize. Several individual Christians count me as a friend, even while the church as a whole condemns me because I repudiated it. I do not take issue with individual Christians (we can agree to disagree), but I have a real problem with the church as an entity. Psychological research has shown that people's viewpoints are magnified when they adopt a fortress mentality (as against the "evils of the world") and stop considering outside information.

The Stanford Prison Experiment in 1971 illustrated this principle by enlisting student volunteers to act as "prison guards" on the one hand and "inmates" on the other. The experiment had to be terminated early because the volunteers—even those who espoused Christian or otherwise high ethical standards—began blatantly violating those standards. The "guards" subjected "prisoners" to humiliating and even sadistic treatment; the role-playing inmates rebelled at this treatment and became unruly, even rioting. They were eventually taken to the police. The high level of stress progressively led them from rebellion to inhibition. By the experiment's end, many showed severe emotional disturbances.

If there is any better representation than the prison experiment of the herd mentality and the abuse it can engender, it is the behavior of the Roman Catholic Church when it enjoyed virtually unchallenged power. It took the role of the prison guards and subjected its "prisoners" to abuse, humiliation, psychological and educational imprisonment, and false accusations.

The bishop Augustine of Hippo, later canonized by the Catholic Church, envisioned a "City of God" on earth where infidels would be "compelled"—or forced—to come in. The rationale? A manipulative misreading of Jesus' parable about the man who can

I want to make one thing clear: I'm not writing this out of some bitterness against the church for having undertaken these actions (though I vigorously condemn them). I believe in living in the present. What I see within the evangelical church as an entity is a desire to appropriate governmental powers to create a "Christian nation" that would, I have no doubt, subject its subjects to the same sort of abuses. I wouldn't want a "Pagan nation" or a "Buddhist nation" for the same reason. The kind of arrogance that invariably results from such situations flies in the face of everything Jesus taught about humility. I see little such humility in the "church" these days, but I do find it in some individual Christians such as my next-door neighbors and a few others. When separated from the "groupthink" defensive and fortress mentality of the church as a whole, they suddenly have "ears to hear" and begin putting such ideals as humility and service before coercion and defensiveness.

One thing that appealed to me about Protestant Christianity was that it purported to offer a "personal relationship" with God rather than requiring a priestly mediator—a church or powerful leader who could easily abuse that power. Sadly, I found that this principle was abandoned in practice once "the church" began formulating dogmas and inserting itself between the believer and God—not just Catholic dogmas, but dogmas like not listening to rock music, not drinking alcohol (even though Jesus turned water into wine!), not dancing, not being sexual ... the list goes on and on. Somehow, the church had entirely undermined everything Jesus was trying to do in superseding the "law that leads to death" and boiling spirituality down to the single principle of love—for God and one's neighbor. The church had created a new set of laws, and the only possible conclusion I could come to was, they stood in direct opposition to Jesus' teachings.

To remain true to those teachings, I had to get out. Ethically, I could not do otherwise. Does this mean I think all groups (such as the church) are bad? No. I believe that, as long as the group's mission is collaborative, it can accomplish amazing things that are more than the sum of its parts, hence, Jesus' promise that his followers would do greater things than he had done. But when the group's focus is to rein in, convert or dominate those outside its bounds, it becomes abusive and destructive, gaining power through intimidation and then seeking to hold it through defensiveness and insecurity. So was the command of Rome that committed monotheists "worship" the emperor. Forced conversions to Islam by the followers of Muhammad is another example of this. The brutal Nazi regime and the imperialistic communism of the USSR are both examples of this. The common thread lies not in the belief system, but in its intent on converting others to its way of thinking, often at all costs. It is not Christianity that leads to groupthink, it is evangelism.

Those who seek to convert others are looking outside themselves. They are those who Jesus mentioned when he admonished his listeners to take the log out of their own eye before they attempt dealing with the speck (or relatively insignificant issue) they find offensive in another. Jesus himself spoke of the answer: "The kingdom of God," he said, was within. Hence, those who focus on finding fault outside of themselves lose touch with this divine reality.

I have found that Pagans often tend to listen more readily than church members, becoming "those who have ears to hear." This does not make Paganism inherently better or worse than Christianity. It is, I believe, primarily the feature of any group that has been targeted by restrictive and abusive behavior on the part of a majority group. If Paganism were to become the national religion, I have no doubt that the same sort of abuse would occur as has been perpetuated by the Christian establishment. I have great respect for Judaism as a religion precisely because it does NOT seek to proselytize or control others; it merely wants to retain the freedom to practice as it sees fit. Isn't that what we all want?

In the end, I left the church in order to follow the example of Jesus. And I found Paganism the most fitting (for me) means of doing so. To the orthodox Jews of his day, Jesus himself was a Pagan— a blasphemer from the country who opposed the rigid religious establishment of his day. I asked myself: If I have ears to hear, how can I do any less?

you know what they say about preachers' kids...

By Jo Lynn Settle Hartwell

MY FATHER WAS A WELL-KNOWN Presbyterian minister who graduated from Bob Jones University, Reformed Theologi-cal Seminary, and received a Doctorate from Westminster Theological Seminary. He was described as a "minister's minister". He actually was one of the founding ministers of his denomination, which split from the Presbyterian Church in the US. My mother also graduated from Bob Jones University with a degree in Speech Education. Her brother and brother-in-law were Free Will Baptist ministers.

Obviously, my upbringing was very Christian oriented. I attended every church service from the time I was born and was even at the church in-between services. I went to every Vacation Bible School as soon as I was old enough and attended Christian summer camps for a few summers. I basically 'accepted Jesus' every summer from about ages 6 to 18. I attended Christian schools if there was one that met my father's approval where we lived. I learned some Greek and Hebrew along the way, and how to ask the hard questions. My father hated those questions.

I asked how are women made in the image of God if he's male? Where did he get the idea for a woman? And why is Wisdom referred to as a woman in the Old Testament but the Holy Spirit in the New? And if Jesus said he came to fulfill the law and the prophets, why do we still obey the rules from the Old Testament? And if the Old Testament is still applicable, why are men not allowed to have more than one wife and why don't we still stone sinners? If God really loved his people, why was he so mean to them all the time? Who did Cain find to marry after he killed Abel and where did they come from? Why was God constantly telling his people to not worship other gods if he is the only one? And if, as Calvin taught, there were a limited number of predestined believers to actually make it to heaven, why even bother striving to be a perfect Christian? If you are counted in that group, wouldn't you get there anyway? And one of the hardest was why would a loving God afflict a young mother with terminal cancer? The answer to that was because through her suffering and death, someone might come to the Lord. I countered with the thought that her suffering and death could possibly drive her sons away from Him.

I'm sure you get the idea: Difficult questions for a man who taught that the Bible was the literal word of God, even if written by men. I'm sure he hated it when I would tell him I had a question. I think I remember him actually flinching a few times.

As I grew up in the fish bowl that is a minister's life, things were even harder for me to accept. I learned early on that 'Christians' could be some of the meanest people. Since I was not allowed many of the same freedoms as other children my age, I never fit in with the youth groups. I never felt accepted and was constantly bullied, but I still tried to meet the expectations of my parents and the church societies I lived in.

Hiding underneath my seeming obedience was a rebellious soul. As I began to let her out, other questions began to be raised and I started searching for answers. To begin with, I did a lot of searching in church-connected arenas. I went from the Calvinist viewpoint to Catholicism. While in the Catholic Church, I discovered their brand of Pentecostalism. That took my search to a non-denominational, Holy Spirit, Word of Faith church. I was once again attending every service and Bible study class. I even taught Bible in their school. Found out they were just as mean and condescending as the Presbyterians and Catholics. And I still did not have answers to my questions but I was willing to bury them for a while.

My family and I left South Carolina for Texas where my dad was one of the ministers at a very wealthy church in Dallas. We settled in a small town east of there and I began the search for a church. There was one that belonged to my father's denomination in our town, but didn't want to go back to that rigidity. I found another small non-denominational church that fit for a while. I became an assistant pastor before it closed down due to the head pastor stealing funds and being overtly handy with some of the girls in a ministry for troubled youth. That left a very sour taste in my mouth and going to church became anathema to me.

Eventually, we moved back to the East Coast. My mother had been diagnosed with early onset Alzheimer's, so when they moved back to South Carolina, we came too. I wanted my girls to have as much time with her while she was alert, and I was tired of the Texas summers. The girls and I decided to settle in a small town west of Asheville, North Carolina, while my husband moved in with his parents in South Carolina, ostensibly so he could do some work for them until he could get a job in North Carolina. Thankfully, he never did! This proved to be a wonderful time of discovery and change for me.

One dark night, as I once again contemplated finding a church, I felt a tug in my soul. A voice calling to my spirit. A reminder that I was a spiritual being. I took time to listen in the days to come. Signs began to come to my attention in lots of little synchronistic ways. I began to ask for wisdom and guidance, which came through Facebook posts about the Goddess. Ads for books speaking about other belief systems and appearing in front of my eyes at Goodwill kept directing me. Reminders showed up in conversations that many Christian holidays began as Pagan and what that meant. I read and journaled and read some more.

I began to realize that many of the issues I had with 'the church' were gone as I accepted the presence of the Goddess. I found a temple in Asheville where I could ask my questions and get real answers. It was wonderful! I truly felt born again. Then my dad found out that I was searching elsewhere for spiritual meaning. He called me to ask what was going on. I told him. He said that because I had been throwing my rebellion in his face all those years that I attended other churches and was now stepping away from his beliefs, I was no longer considered his child and could not see my mother anymore. I calmly stated that I appreciated this shining example of unconditional love that he had preached all my life. I said good-bye and hung up.

Shortly after this, I received a call from my aunt that my mother was in the hospital and dying. My youngest daughter and I drove to her bedside so we could say our farewells. My father refused to give me any private time with her and proceeded to preach a sermon at me across my mother's deathbed. The funeral was much of the same hell and damnation without Jesus that I had heard all my life, but my spirit constantly reminded me that this was their circus, not mine.

Due to my mind being opened by the Goddess, I also came to know that I was a lesbian. I had blocked from my memory intimate times with a friend in my late teens because of the whole Jesus thing and trying to get the approval of my father by marrying a penis. The Goddess brought these memories flooding back and another part of me was born again. Since I accepted the call of the Goddess and have pursued Her as she pursued me, my spirit is now at home in my life. I am no longer running and hiding from the truth inside me. The Ancient Mother has pulled me into her embrace and shown me who I really am.

Jo Lynn Settle Hartwell was born in West Virginia in 1961. Mother of two independent feminist daughters and grandmother to a female force of nature. My wife and I recently moved to Portugal, where the Ancient Mother is continuing to speak to me.

coming home to the goddess

By Amy Hillecke (Cetryn)

MY FATHER WAS RAISED CATHOLIC, attending Catholic school through 8th grade. His entire family has been Catholic for generations and is immersed in a strongly Catholic community. My mother was raised Baptist. Her family, especially on her mother's side (including my eldest uncle and his nuclear family) is very involved in their churches. Her best friend (through whom my parents met) was also Catholic. My parents' wedding was at my father's church, after convincing the priest that they truly believed they would make their religious differences work.

Despite all the Christianity that saturated their lives, my parents decided not to raise their kids in the church. We were never baptized. Our extended families did send us plenty of Christian Primer books, and would take us to their Easter sermons or find one local to us when they were visiting. And of course, we sang the Christmas Carols and learned those stories. But it wasn't *the* Truth for us.

About the time I started school, my parents joined a Group that focused on metaphysics. I believe at least two of the leaders/members were predominantly Native American. The Group explored things like spirit guides, auras, crystal energy, healing touch, astral projection, dreamwalking, things like that. Meetings always included guided group meditation. Kids were welcome to participate or just play quietly in the next room.

At the same time, my best friend and I devoured information about Greek, Roman, Egyptian, and Norse mythologies.

Throughout my school years, we lived in a heavily Mormon area and I developed several friendships with members of that church. I was invited to join them at church but my parents denied me that experience because of the cult they knew it to be (largely based on the word of my mom's brother-in-law who was excommunicated).

As I approached adolescence, the Group welcomed a couple who were initiated Wiccans who were, for the sake of enlightenment, invited to teach the Group about Wicca. My sister and I were especially intrigued and continued to take teachings from the couple, including starting our own Books of Shadow and participating in a Maidenhood Ceremony.

In my early high school years I started dating a longtime friend who happened to be very active in his own church. At the time, his life dream was to become a pastor. He invited me to join him at his church and in his youth group with his other friends. For the better part of a year, I participated multiple times a week and discussed the lessons with him. I had a lot of catching up to do to learn the stories, having not really been brought up in it. I read a lot of Christian fiction, motivational texts, and several chapters of The Bible (in various versions, since I had copies of Catholic and Baptist Bibles, and now newer modern versions). I enjoyed Genesis and Exodus, and much of the New Testament (including the real history surrounding it). I was especially enamored with Revelations, and dove into a great deal of debate surrounding Leviticus.

I was embracing both and theology and lifestyle, listening to Country and Christian Rock almost exclusively. I never fully got away from seeing everything as a form of mythology, but I did see it as a more plausible explanation of "things" than those proposed by the other mythologies I had studied. For all intents and purposes, I was doing everything I could to prepare myself to be a pastor's wife.

Until the Sunday before Halloween.

That Sunday the pastor's sermon largely revolved around the evils of Halloween. He went on and on about the devil's temptation and the dangers posed by Satan's disciples, including attempts they made on the life of children or going so far as to kidnap children to sacrifice them to their dark lord. But what really rubbed me the wrong way was how the pastor used the terms Satanist, Wiccan, Cultist, and Pagan interchangeably. Having so recently explored them firsthand, I knew for a fact that Wiccans and Pagans did no such things. But seeing the rest of the congregation taking that all in, and nodding along, I had no voice to correct them. Instead, I curled up quietly in my corner.

After the service, I discussed it with my boyfriend. He acknowledged what I was saying, but I could see that he still saw Wicca as devil-worship and had doubts to my ability to truly embrace Christianity. I had lost all respect for that pastor, and could no longer bring myself to attend their church.

I tried to continue participating in the youth group and Bible studies but I never was able to shake the experience of such willful ignorance and, for lack of a better word, hatred.

I think my boyfriend's family picked up on this because shortly thereafter my boyfriend broke up with me, saying his mom wouldn't allow the relationship to continue. I was devastated. I stopped all Christian activities. The only thing that continued was the occasional debate with Christian friends about their practices and texts.

About that time, my best friend brought me to a new craft shop that had opened up in town. The owners were Pagans of the old tradition, having previously lived in the UK where the man had grown up. Among their craft supplies, they offered wands, athames, crystal balls, images of the Goddess and her Consort and other such paraphernalia. Their youngest son was my age, and quickly became a close friend. We celebrated the Sabbats together and generally embraced everything Pagan. We, along with other friends, discovered a great many Pagan musicians, too, across many genres. We even stood up for our religious freedom and representation at school.

I've never looked back at Christianity. It took me years to get over the abandonment I felt from my former love—despite our continuing friendship—but it was nothing compared to the *rightness* I felt in being Pagan. I have continued to research other religions, including the various sects of Christianity and Abrahamic religions, as well as Eastern, Indigenous, and ancient European traditions, and participate in friendly philosophical discussions on related topics. Overall, all of the research and discourse has only contributed to my eclecticism, but at the root of it all, I largely embrace the Wiccan traditions that gave a sturdy framework upon which to build.

a very different calling

By David Moore

Y MOTHER BEGAN TEACHING ME TO read as soon as I was able to sit up on my own. She would bring a flash card to where I was playing, get my attention, and point her finger: "Look! God! G-O-D. God." Then she would walk away as quickly as she had approached. When I was three, she overheard me 'reciting' a Dick and Jane story. She looked in, and was surprised to see me actually reading a book aloud. She exclaimed, "You can READ?" I answered, "Mommy, we have been reading together for a long time." She had no idea I was fully aware of all of our reading and was following along.

My parents were devout Jehovah's Witnesses. Unlike many of the things you may have heard, Jehovah's Witnesses have a very Bible-centric faith. Originally called International Bible Students, they began as scholars and kept their scholarly methodology to this day. I was steeped in study and learning, and at the age of five I was enrolled in their Theocratic Ministry School. I was taught public speaking, teaching, and how to prepare and deliver Bible-themed talks. By the time I was six, I was doing it all on my own. We were a clergy tradition, evangelical to the core, and preaching was a way of life. We constantly heard the charge, "Go, therefore, and make disciples of people of all the nations"—and believe me, we all tried. While others thought we were nuts for our level of dedication, we saw ourselves as working hard to follow the commandments of our maker—and that simply wasn't too much to do. It was the least we could do in return for life.

I was doing the work of Christian clergy before I was enrolled in kindergarten. I taught Bible studies, gave talks at our meetings, and went out preaching from door to door, answering questions and challenges deftly, very skilled with my Bible and reasoning ability.

I helped people who needed counseling and spent a lot of personal time in prayer and research.

After what was enough study to earn more than one PhD in Biblical and religious studies, in total about 40,000 actual hours, I decided that what I had wasn't the "truth" I had always been told it was. I had major problems with the idea of setting humans up for failure and then punishing them. I had huge issues with punishing innocent children for what their parents did, much more their ancient ancestors. A death sentence is harsh, and when passed on to future generations, it is just intolerably evil. Destroying the world in a huge flood isn't okay either, under any circumstance, and tolerating the wicked behavior still going on in the world today is NOTHING like loving. I couldn't accept that a god of love was 'jealous' (an emotional sickness rather than a virtue), and prone to deadly outbursts. I had to find the truth of the nature of God, and I didn't care what the Bible said about deity—I needed to discover my own truth, one that my kind heart could accept and love.

I broke away from their religion, which nearly broke my father's heart. He was absolutely sick over it and didn't speak to me for years. We had been very close so that was just as devastating to me. My mother had always been afflicted with a mental disorder—physically abusive and also mentally and emotionally abusive. I didn't care as much what she thought of it. No matter what the cost, I could not kowtow to such a deity again. It offended my conscience (the conscience people had no right to in the first place, according to the story of Adam and Eve, but that's another topic for discussion).

I bought books by Anton Szandor LaVey, but I soon realized that he was merely a disillusioned Christian who was lashing out in a childish rebellion, seeking attention in his circus-instilled way and looking to take advantage of others. I hadn't found an alternative view that made sense. I was encouraged to study Buddhism by my first Kung Fu teacher, and he helped me make my first altar. It featured a statue of Ho Tai in the center (the fat, bald guy many think is Buddha but is a Chinese pioneer who brought Buddhism to China). On the right side, it had a male Chinese bust, and on the left side a female one, featuring matching blue traditional peasant tops, with the frog buttons. He and I crawled on the ground in Georgia's red clay, searching for white sand grains. Eventually, we did find enough of them to fill my little cauldron, which was for burning incense sticks. We had to find enough grains so that sticks of incense would stand up on their own. I'll never forget the difficulty involved with the tradition he passed along. All of our efforts notwithstanding, although I appreciated the teachings of the compassionate Buddha as I received them, I didn't find myself there. I loved the altar and the symbolism but my search continued.

I began to date a girl who was to become the mother of my first child, a son. One day when she was in the other room, I was browsing her bookshelf (I always was a bookworm, as you may recall), and I saw a pamphlet entitled, "The Charge of the Goddess." I was fascinated instantly, and absorbed it by the time she entered the room again. I just kept reading and rereading it as I quizzed her for answers about it. I was enthralled. She offered to take me to a meeting with some witches, and I have never looked back. We met at a small mobile home in Warner Robins, Georgia, barely twelve or thirteen of us. A third-degree high priestess was driving two hours from her home in Atlanta to teach us and work with us here. Outwardly, we were called Rainbow Wreath, but our "inner circle" name was Silver Web. In my very first circle I met my God and Goddess for the first time in person, and I was changed forever. We often say, "She changes everything she touches;" I was touched, and that was that. She was really there and so was He. Nothing like that had happened to me in a church environment before. FINALLY, I felt the benevolence and kindness I just knew had to be behind this universe. Answers were flooding in, and I was on my way—but Wicca wasn't the whole pie for me. I was meant for something different.

Although I continued my studies after my second degree, for a variety of reasons I always stopped short of my third degree ritual, and that happened with three teachers. What was holding me back? I didn't necessarily find myself agreeing with all of the tenets, couldn't imagine myself teaching others things I didn't personally believe, and didn't find that there was enough structure and organization to ensure quality control in the learning environment. Chaos reigned, and personal egos abounded and clashed. I loved witchcraft, to be sure, but I could tell that what I was learning wasn't exactly my personal journey. Also, my studies often uncovered common misconceptions that were being taught at a growing rate globally to those earnestly seeking witchcraft. However, I had met my

Mother! I grew up knowing about a heavenly Father, but was missing the comforting and loving bosom of my Mother until I met her in that circle and dedicated myself to Her.

After years of introspection, a foray into polyamory and lots of reading, I finally came to the conclusion that I can never turn my back on my Lord and Lady, no matter my religious inclination. The study and focus on love was the ultimate hike through wonder. I also cherished the concept of love as an ultimate truth and goodness. I came to believe whole-souled that LOVE was the nature of the universe and the right answer to every question. When asked now, I simply say that my religion is Love. My basic belief is that love is the only good motivation for anything, so it provides a fine moral filter for deciding our actions. "Do I want to do this for a loving reason? Will it have a loving result? Will it cause more benefit or harm to individuals and the collective of humanity?" and so on.

Along the way, one full moon night around sixteen years ago as of this writing, after casting a circle, I laid down on my back on the cracked asphalt of an abandoned tennis court. I gazed at her fullness and brightness, and I earnestly implored my Lord and Lady, my Father and Mother, to tell me what I was supposed to do. I thanked them for their love and guidance, and I asked them what I could possibly do to show them my appreciation. What could I contribute? Their faces appeared to me, and smiled. Each of their heads was as big as the full moon in the sky. I couldn't hear them speak when their mouths moved, but I was shown things and the meaning was clear. They showed me a book, and a pen. I asked, "Am I supposed to write something?" They both nodded at me. "What am I supposed to write?" They explained, partly in pictures and partly nearly audibly and somehow understood, that I was to clear up misconceptions, show people the truth, and help guide their children back to them. HOW was such a monumental task to be accomplished, I wondered. What a huge thing. How could ANY book do that?

They left that for me to discover, but I had been given a clear assignment. What would I do with it? The brainstorming period lasted years. I asked other people, reflected inwardly, and despaired. Elders in the community would just discredit me if I said anything contrary to their teachings, I thought. Younger people would wonder what my credentials were, to be writing such things. I would need to do a LOT of searching to even think I had such truths to tell. Who was I to take on such a task? But… I hadn't been taught fear of men as a youth. I had been taught to boldly and fearlessly go forth and do my duty. Here was a duty assigned to me, so regardless of any haters, I had to move on it. I really sank into my studies and began conceptualizing a plan to create the effect they described to me. I am still working on it today, but it's almost a finished manuscript now. I have no idea whether it will do what they said—I just have to finish it, then close my eyes and trust that it'll at least help someone. I'm scared sometimes, feel inadequate a lot of times, and have called upon various elders to guide me and answer questions for an appendix, so they could weigh in on various topics.

Someday you will see a book on the shelf. It will be entitled, *Banishing the Shadows—Revealing the Truth in Witchcraft and Pagan Religion.* You will know that it was born from a late-night session gazing at the full moon. You will know that although I feel inadequate to deliver it, it has a higher purpose. Pick it up, thumb through it, and see if any of it calls to you. I hope so, because They are waiting for us to return to Them, and They want us to know the Truth.

David Moore, called Krodin by his fellow witches, was first initiated as a witch in 1992. His travels across the globe and intense studies from a young age make him a very unusual mix: Bible scholar cum Pagan writer/teacher. Book nerd meets naturalist, a devoutly religious man with no religious label, he teaches private classes and spends time editing Pagan books and writing his own work when not working by day as an electrician.

I found Wicca

By Patricia Winkler

I DO HAVE A STORY ABOUT MY FLIGHT FROM the Lutheran Church (now Evangelical Church in America – ELCA Synod). Mom and Dad had me baptized and christened Lutheran (he was lapsed Catholic, and she was Christian Science, lapsed). I was brought up in the Lutheran Church (the whole ritual, Sunday School, Choir member, Sunday School teacher and eventually a council member). I became a member of the Council after my father died (my mother was also a member). I was about 21 or 22 and eventually became a member of the Stewardship committee. This was the committee in charge of getting people to pledge their donations (not strict about tithing) so the church could plan the year to come's budget. The church I belonged to would send out pledge cards for each member family/single person to fill out. Then on Pledge Sunday everyone would go to the front of the church to place their pledge cards in the offering plates. It was a day of great rejoicing. I thought it was so cool.

Then the Stewardship committee had its meeting afterward and members who had not filled out a card were documented and then I found out the Lutheran Church's dirty little secret. There was a thing called Visitation Sunday and members of the Council would team up and go out to the homes of people who had not filled out a Pledge Card and try to get them to fill one out. We would carry blanks in case a person or family had not received their card in the group mailing.

I was appalled. I even asked the other members if they would provide me with a blackjack so I could perhaps force the filling out of the cards. I swear, I felt like I was working as an enforcer for an organization not far removed from the Mafia. That was it, I walked away. I went on the visitation with my mother and then I resigned from the council. Tried out different religions for a while and then found Wicca. That was in 1986 and have been practicing ever since.

the pagan heart ~ a reflection

By AnnaLisa Wiley

A S A YOUNG CHILD, I LIVED IN THE BIG cities of the east coast. My early religious education was Lutheran Christianity. When I was seven, my mother remarried and we moved to a more rural area of upstate New York. As part of my education, my stepfather introduced me to his Native American friends, which gave me an appreciation of history and the natural environment that would not be found in my textbooks.

I invite you now to come with me as I run across the wide lawn to the path that runs between the woods and the cornfield. Find the break in bushes and duck under branches of the two large elm trees at the edge of the woods. The canopy is thick and cool here with little underbrush. The woods are filled with oak and elm, sugar maple and sycamore. Breathe deep, smelling the wild flowers and the soft fragrant compost of leaf fall.

Walk softly, listening for the birdcalls telling you that you are safe. Try to pass through the forest without making a sound like Dad says the Indians can, and wonder how they avoided the twigs that occasionally crack under your bare feet. See the fallen decaying log where the tiny red salamanders live. Look up and see the nests of the birds high above you.

Slow to a walk as your feet slide in the mud under a layer leaves and down a steep embankment that leads to an old logging trail. Break into a run and move quickly down a slope until you see a smaller trail off to your left. It's a narrow one that asks you to bend under branches and step over logs. Look close and see the tracks of the white-tailed deer, a dangerous animal with their multi-tined antlers, but so beautiful and very gentle. You top a rise and look down into the ravine and now you can see it.

The Deer Pond. It is a small pond, mostly in shadow since the trees grow nearly to the water's edge. An old tree has fallen into it and has started to rot and you inch yourself along it, closer to the center of the pond.

Sit down. Relax.

See the algae that forms a layer of green lace around the edges of the water. Watch the butterflies and the dust motes in the sunbeams that break through trees overhead. Let your eyes relax and your vision blur a bit. Can you see the fairies skating on the water?

On the far side of the pond, a young buck approaches; he sniffs the air, You hold very still because he is downwind and can't see you well. Gracefully, he dips his head to drink. The breeze shifts, he catches your scent and bounds off, white tail raised like a flag of peace.

Sitting there you know that everything is right with the world, that this world is *alive*, and you are as much a part of it as the deer and the butterfly and the pond.

This was my special place. It prepared me to recognize the Goddess when I encountered her in later life and formed a sanctuary from the insanity of my later childhood.

From age of ten until I was 19, I studied Mormonism and did my best to be as perfect as they implied I could be. That gave way to atheism but my belief in the mystical prevailed. When I turned back to formal religion, I allowed a friend to drag me into a Pentecostal church where I was "born again." If any of you have had a friend get caught up in that...bible thumping frenzy, well, mine's the same story. Finally I mellowed out and ended up back in the Lutheran Church where I had spent my early years. There I was blessed and assisted in my spiritual growth until the late '80s when I started reading books like Merlin Stone's *When God Was a Woman* and Zimmer-Bradley's *The Mists of Avalon.*

I took courses in Social Psychology and Comparative Mythology and started attending Wiccan and Native America rituals. These rituals and the teachers that led them opened a door to realms that gave deeper meaning to my early woodland experiences. The age-old prejudice that crept into Christianity during the dark ages drove a wedge between the lessons of my Pagan teachers and my Christian congregation. My mind and spirit felt the conflict. The more I learned, the more I studied, the more the conflict grew. Nothing made sense. Nature, even in winter when the deer starved and the ponds froze, always made sense.

Experience taught me that whether we like the answer or not, the answer to a prayer will always come. At that point I didn't care what the answer was, I just wanted an answer. I prayed long and hard, sure that the answer would be something complex and profound. My heart was heavy. I finally I took a day and went off to pray in the hills in Nature, where the answers had always come more clearly. When it seemed like the answer would never come, I sat on the hillside, crying. A strong breeze blew through the trees. It sounded like a woman's laughter followed by a voice, "He's my *son*, silly."

I just started laughing. It was so obvious. One of the things that Paganism teaches us is to trust our own, intuitive knowledge, to understand that we are one with the Earth. Everything that sustains our bodies comes from the Earth who, absorbing the energy of the Sun, provides us with warmth, food, water and air. We are *all* children of the Goddess: you, me, Jesus, Mary, Buddha, even Dick Cheney!

Not just us two-legged, either. The four-leggeds, the winged ones, those with flippers and fins—we are all children of the Earth.

My Christian friends were hurt and confused by my expanding beliefs. After a while, I knew didn't belong there anymore, but forty years of relying on Biblical teachings also made it difficult to fit into available Pagan groups. Then, and even now, there is strong anti-Christian sentiment among those who cannot forgive the atrocities that were committed in the name of "Christ." It would be another ten years before someone invited me to attend services at a Unitarian Universalist congregation, where no one is compelled to "correct" my beliefs even when they think my ideas are totally absurd.

I have tried to share a fraction of what Paganism means to me. It is less a prescribed set of beliefs and more a feeling, a deep connectedness to all life. It is what we strive for as Unitarian Universalists when

"We covenant to affirm and promote....

Respect for the interdependent web of all existence of which we are a part."

from christian to pagan

By Samina Ocean

MY NAME IS SAMINA OCEAN, AND I live in Las Vegas. Most of my life I have been in the entertainment business in one form or another. Here is my story of how I went from Christianity to where I am today.

My mother's side of the family was Quaker when they first came to American but had converted to Methodism. My father of Italian heritage was raised Catholic, but as a singer his only interest in going to church was singing in the choir.

I was baptized Methodist and was reluctantly dragged to church every Sunday to sit on an uncomfortable bench in an uncomfortable dress, trying to sing boring songs in a key that was always too high, and then try to stay awake while this man spouted off a sermon that I could never understand.

It was hard for my mother go get my dad to go to church so she switched us to Episcopalian (Catholic light). She thought that this compromise would make it easier to get my father to go more often.

Now, along with all of the other boring stuff, we had to add uncomfortable kneeling, eating these awful wafers and sipping terrible wine. On Easter I would choke on the horrible incense that the priest would wave in a big burner.

When I was 15 my mother was killed in a plane crash, so my dad's mother, Grandma Betty, came to live with us. She had become a born-again Christian but even with the evils that were taught about witchcraft, it was my grandmother who first introduced me to methods of divination like the pendulum.

My mother had been the structure and rule-maker of the house. Once she was gone, I had no parental supervision. My father was always more of a friend than a parent, as was my grandmother. Our house and lives began to be in disarray.

Around six months after my mother's death I was awakened out of a dead sleep with the sound of her voice calling my name. I rolled over to see a shadow standing by my bed. I was so shocked and scared that I pulled the covers over my head and said, "Go away!" To this day I regret that reaction.

In the morning I thought it was all just a dream. I was distraught by my mother's untimely passing and what I had seen and heard couldn't have been real.

A couple of days later, my friend's mother, Mary, called my grandmother and asked if she and I could come over. When we arrived, Mary asked us to sit down, and began by saying that we may not believe what she was about to tell us, but she had to.

Mary said that she was able to communicate to souls who have passed over. She said that my mother had visited her, and was deeply upset, and crying. She appeared to her dressed in pants and a sleeveless shirt, with her hair pulled back.

My mother asked for Mary's help, because she said "evil" was trying to get into her home and that her family was falling apart. She told Mary my brother was stealing, my sister was lost, and my dad and I were at odds with each other. It was all true!

The only thing that my grandmother thought to do was to get us all to go to church with her. If I hadn't seen the spirit of my mother first-hand I probably wouldn't have gone, so I was off with my grandmother to become a born-again Christian.

Mary kept us informed of my mother's visits, which for a while were the same. In a few months we started to pull back together as a family, and that is when my mother came to Mary dressed in a beautiful white gown with her hair down and flowing. She thanked Mary for her help, and said that if she ever needed anything to ask.

For almost two years, I tried to be the best Christian I could be. I quit drugs, sex and all of the other things that a "good Christian" should not do. I went to church every Sunday, and also on Wednesdays to a program for teens called Maranatha.

I wanted desperately to have what the preacher said I could have, to be consumed by the Holy Spirit and "talk in tongues." I wanted this with all of my being, but there was something that just wasn't right.

My suspicions began when I went up to the altar to receive the spirit of Jesus Christ. I had seen so many go up and fall under the power of the Holy Spirit. I waited with anticipation for Reverend Sharp to get to me. I saw person after person falling backward in trance, with someone there to catch them.

When it was my turn, the catcher stood behind me and Reverend Sharp said, "Receive the power of Jesus Christ!" He then pushed so hard against my forehead that I did fall backward, but I felt nothing else. I lay there for a minute wondering what had just happened. Was I just not worthy?

This prompted many questions about my journey as a Christian. I was so confused. I went to the elders who were running the Maranatha program and asked for their help. I told them of my mother's death and how she appeared to me and then to my friend's mother.

Their first reaction was to tell me firmly that what I saw was not my mother, but Satan. It was evil trying to lead me astray. I then asked them if they were absolutely positive about this, and they said yes, spirits cannot appear to you, it was of Satan! I said, "Really, because it was that spirit that led me here, so you must be of Satan!"

I did go back to church a couple more times, but with a different perspective. I saw Reverend Sharp as a performer and hypnotist casting his suggestions to the masses and all of the willing recipients falling under his spell.

What Christianity had to offer was not for me.

Around 1989 when I was in my early thirties a friend brought me to a quaint little occult shop called Bell, Book & Candle. Through this shop I learned about candle magic, spells and all the lovely things that go along with being a witch. It felt right and made sense to me to be in sync with the earth, moon, and stars, and to not be afraid of what lies beyond the shadows or beyond the veil.

The owner of the shop, Lucky, invited me to my first full moon circle led by Raymond Buckland, who was well-known in the occult world. I waited with anticipation as we circled up around the altar, but I was very disappointed with the ritual. It was just as boring as sitting in church, just too rigid and solemn for my taste. I only went to one other full moon ritual. I was on the path of a solitary witch.

One day when I was in Bell, Book & Candle, I was looking at the many photos of entertainers who had visited the shop. Lucky asked me if I knew one of the faces on the wall, Jeff McBride. I said that I didn't, which surprised Lucky because he was a well-known stage magician who practiced "real" magic as well. At the time I, too, was in both magic worlds. I became a magician's assistant when I was 18 and then became a magician myself. I knew all the big-name magicians in Las Vegas, but not Jeff.

A couple of weeks later I was talking to one of the well-known magicians and he also mentioned Jeff McBride. I said, "Who is this guy, Jeff McBride?" He said the same thing Lucky had said, "I can't believe you don't know him. You need to know Jeff McBride!"

A month later I saw a billboard announcing a well-known entertainer who would be playing at the Golden Nugget hotel. Opening for the entertainer was Jeff McBride! I almost ran off the road. This was literally a sign from the universe!

On opening night, I sent Jeff a bouquet of flowers to his dressing room, with a card explaining how I knew Lucky and Lance and how they both told me that I needed to know him. After the show, I called Jeff backstage to see if he got the flowers and to further introduce myself. He seemed a little hesitant, but invited me to come see the show the next night. I gladly accepted.

Jeff's style of magic was different than any I had seen before. After the show, we went out to dinner and then up to his hotel room, where he blew my mind with some close-up magic of which I had never seen before either. He had combined the esoteric with the usual magic I had grown bored with. This was exciting!

At the time Jeff lived in NY where he had begun something a year before called Mystery School, a week-long adventure combining both esoteric magick and stage magic. In a few months I was off to Goshen NY. While I was there I heard of an event called the Spiral Gathering in GA that Jeff was going to. I felt compelled to attend.

A whole other world opened up with different kinds of ritual and mysteries, along with dancing and drumming around a sacred fire. I was hooked! But I told Jeff that I needed to find my spiritual fix on the west coast. He told me I needed to know Katlyn Miller, who also was into both magic worlds and had attended the first Mystery School. She had just moved to Las Vegas from Long Beach, California, with her new husband.

We met up a month or so later and became fast friends. I went with Kat to many OTO rituals in the Long Beach area, including the Eleusinian Mysteries—an amazing adventure!

One day Katlyn called me and said that she wanted to create a circle here in Las Vegas. Of course, I said yes! This was Desert Moon Circle which has been going strong since 1994.

At first I had no idea what I was doing, but I learned quickly with on-the-job priestess training, following in Katlyn's footsteps. I brought drumming and the many chants I had learned from my time with Jeff and his now-wife Abigail Spinner McBride. We molded DMC into an eclectic circle of celebration and joy.

After one of our rituals, a woman came up to me and told me that she had never experienced anything like it before. She said that all of the other rituals she had attended were solemn and rigid (just like my first one). She told me she was moved by the joy that was on my face as I opened the circle and sang in the quarters. Yes, to me, this is how it should be!

DMC had been in full swing for six years when Katlyn decided to do an initiation into the priesthood for myself, our acting priest Bob, his wife Norma, and one other acting priestess, Karen.

Jeff McBride had now been living in Las Vegas for a few years and had attended many DMC rituals. Katlyn got together with Jeff and Abigail to put together a life-altering initiation. I cannot get into a lot of the details. I can tell you that we were blindfolded and driven to a secret place. I sat for quite some time in meditation, still blindfolded, and then was led on a journey of trust.

At one point I was led up a few stairs, asked to cross my arms across my chest and fall backward. I did with no hesitation; I knew there would be people there to catch me. Then I was stopped by the sound of a sword being unsheathed and felt the tip of its blade against my solar plexus. A powerful woman's voice said, "It is better to fall upon this blade, than to enter into this sacred space in fear. How do you enter?" My answer, "In perfect love, and perfect trust!"

As the blindfold was removed, I saw standing before me a real wizard who asked me to explain the eight spokes of the Wheel of the Year. I had prepared something, as I was told this would happen. When I was finished, the wizard said, "It is done," and the priestess whose blade I had felt upon my solar plexus said, "And done well!"

This was how I first met Oberon and Morning Glory Zell. You can't even imagine how honored I was that Katlyn and Jeff had flown them in to be a part of this life-changing event! I am proud to have become friends with them both and shared many magical times around the sacred fire at festivals and in their home.

fROm now 'til the haRvest comes home

By Steven Posch

I JUST GOT AN INVITATION TO WRITE FOR AN anthology with the cheeky title of *Goodbye Jesus, I'm Going Home to Mother.* It is to be, I gather, a book of tales: "faith journeys" from Jesus to the Goddess.

("Faith journey" is the polite name for "I've changed my mind.")

Inveterate storyteller though I am, I don't (on my own recognizance) really have much of a tale to tell on that account. For me—Christian only by virtue of infant baptism—the story is one not so much of flight *from* as of journey *to*. I fell in love, and that was that. As for so many with whom I speak, my own coming to the Old Ways is a tale more of homecoming than departure.

In those days, mind you, if you wanted the Lady, you had to quest for her. Thinking back, I'm reminded of Robert Graves' own trailblazing search:

> *It was a virtue not to stay: to go my headstrong and heroic way, seeking Her out at the volcano's head, among pack ice, and where the track had faded beyond the cavern of the Seven Sleepers.*

Her we sought everywhere, the Living Goddess—history, geography, folklore—and everywhere we looked, we found her. How not, since all life is a journey to her? From her we come, in her we live, to her we return. Indeed, there's nowhere else to go.

As for Jesus, I don't have much to say, except that—so far as I can tell—we know, and can know, very little about the historical Jesus of Nazareth, and that therefore all Jesuses—and one really does have to speak in the plural here—are essentially fictional characters. I can see little point in addressing him, not even to say goodbye. *Return to sender, addressee deceased.*

So I'll tell you no tales of Jesus. I'm now in my seventh decade, closer to death than birth. Time is dear, and if I were never to hear even one more word about the pale Galilean, I'd still have heard too many.

But tell me instead of Earth and her secrets, of the Moon and her mysteries, of the Sea and her deeps; of Thunder and Sun, of the piping of the Horned, and the Green One's merry dance.

Speak to me of these, my friend, and I'll sit at your feet and listen, rapt, from now till the Harvest comes home.

Poet, master ritualist, and storyteller Steven Posch (1955-) was raised by white-tailed deer in the hardwood forests of western Pennsylvania. (That's the story, anyway.) Current keeper of the Minnesota Ooser, he lives and writes in Minneapolis. He also looks pretty good in a kilt.
https://witchesandpagans.com/pagan-culture-blogs/paganistan.html

my conversion from christianity to paganism

By Taliesin Crow

I WAS RAISED IN A VERY PENTECOSTAL FAMILY, with two uncles and two great uncles who were preachers. I was even convinced from an early age that I was called to be a preacher myself. But I was always been drawn to and intrigued by Norse and Greek mythology. In my rebellious teenage years I experimented with the occult and Satanism, playing with Ouija boards and astral projection and other things. In my late 20s I gave my life back over to Christianity, and tried to walk "the straight and narrow path".

When I was 32 my wife of twelve years left me for a friend of ours, taking our three daughters. My uncle, who was only nine years older than I and was the closest person to me in the whole world, died of a sudden massive heart attack. I wound up in jail because of my ex-wife and ended up having to sign over my parental rights to my children. My ex wanted to cut me out of my children's lives forever because she didn't want them to know that she had been cheating on me with their new "dad." So at a very low point in my life, as usual I reached out to God and Jesus. But I felt nothing, as if my prayers were just empty words heard by nothing or no one.

During this time I had gall bladder problems, and ended up having my gall bladder taken out. But the surgeons made a mistake and left one of my bile ducts open, which then dumped poison directly into my body. I ended up in the hospital on the verge of death. It was on my first night in the hospital when I was closest to death that I had the strangest experience of my life.

While lying in my hospital bed that night, I suddenly felt myself floating above my bed. I opened my eyes to see my body still on the bed. In an instant I was no longer in the hospital bed, but standing in a grassy field. Looking over my left shoulder I saw a cave entrance, and an old woman standing at the entrance to the cave.

Just then a very large black dog came out of the cave, and by very large I mean his head was over six feet tall. I turned around and started running away from the cave. I could hear the dog behind me, and I felt its mouth come down over my left shoulder as if it was going to pick me up. Just as I felt the mouth clamp down on my shoulder, I sat up in the hospital bed in a panic. I would have passed this off as just a dream, but I could still feel its breath on my neck and his teeth on my shoulder.

A year later I met my current wife. I was a bit unsure of her when we met because she was Pagan. But after I told her the story of the woman at the cave and the large dog, she showed me the story of Hel and Garm.

I was floored. In Norse mythology the Valkyries take the souls of those who died bravely in combat, but Hel and her hound Garm take the souls of the old and the sick. I had been most definitely sick, to the point of death. So after a life lived as a Christian, when I came close to death it wasn't Jesus or a white light at the end of a tunnel or my grandparents that I saw, it was a Pagan Goddess.

I have always had questions about Christianity that no one could ever answer, such as, "What about all of the people who died after Christ's death that never heard of him dying for their sins?" such as the Native Americans, African tribes in the middle of a remote jungle in 1500 AD, the Vikings, Japanese, and on and on and on. How many people lived and died after Christ's death, that never could have known that he died for their sins, and so never got to accept him as their personal savior, and so (according to Christians) went to hell? That never sat well at all with me.

But after asking countless pastors, and bishops and elders in the church, my new wife gave me the answer I had always been searching for.

Deity is like a tree. Every branch is a different religion. They all are a part of the same deity. So whether someone worships the Christian God or the Muslim Allah or a Pagan God or Goddess, they are all still serving the same Deity.

It was then that I felt comfortable enough to let go of the dogmas that I had been raised with my entire life and felt free to embrace the Gods and Goddesses of the mythologies I had been so interested in for my entire life. I give special attention to Hel so that if we should meet again, I won't fear her.

from son of god to mother earth

By Tim Workman, Rev. Sylvanus Treewalker

MY RELIGIOUS UPBRINGING WAS basically freeform. I had a friend whose father was a Methodist minister and on occasion I would attend services. Then in my later years I found Christianity as a convert to Pentecostalism via The Church of God, Cleveland, TN, the original snake handlers in America. I attended Church and over time I even aspired to the clergy, but never really pursued it. I had conversations with the pastor and had many questions that never really were answered.

I moved and in my new surroundings I made friends with an ex-Satanist turned Pagan, who in 1993 invited me to his coven's Samhain ritual at our local state park. A friend and I sat on the hood of his car as we watched the ritual. At first I was scared; I thought Satan would get me. But as they danced and sang something just clicked. After ritual we were invited to their campfire and I met the coven members and its priestess and priest.

I was invited to attend a drumming that following week. I started attending classes, rituals and other events, then after a period of time I was initiated into Greenleaf Coven. The Gods and Goddesses were and are an important part of my life.

Looking deeper beyond the dualist concepts of Wicca, I found Pantheist Druidry. Soon I joined Tony Taylor's Henge of Keltria. Two years later I founded The Order of the Standing Oak.

I was an occult book reviewer for Red Wheel/Weiser and hosted Pagan Perspectives on BlogTalkRadio. I interviewed Mike Nichols, Gavin Frost, Selena Fox, Raymond Buckland and Raven Grimassi.

My gratitude to the ancestors, the Gods and the Earth Mother never diminish, and am always moving ahead in the community. I teach, and produce Pagan videos for my YouTube channel, APaganperspective.

As for Jesus, I see him as a prophet, just one God among many.

To his clergy, I say learn and live and love with your beliefs.

And for the Goddess, she is indeed Alive…

the devil's got you, little girl!

By Nicki Ojeda

I LOVE JESUS CHRIST! PUT ANOTHER DIME IN THE offering, mister!" I remember singing that little ditty to the tune of Joan Jett's "I Love Rock n' Roll." One thing I always loved about church was the music. I still find some of it very moving. The first song I ever learned to play on the piano was "Amazing Grace". My grandmother was jealous when I picked it up at about age seven in one hour. She had been practicing it for a week already. Some time later, years, actually, it dawned on me that it might be pathological, her jealousy of her grandchild.

Yes, it was the music that gave me the "feelings" when I went to the altar crying and got "saved." The music made me feel a higher power. I wanted to have Jesus in my heart. And boy, did I drink the Kool-Aid! My family and I sat around the table at night, listening to all the songs with "back-masking," wherein playing popular, mostly rock, songs backwards supposedly reveals their hidden Satanic messages. My cousin and I would be half-scared out of our wits trying to sleep at night after hearing those super-creepy tapes.

I remember being so scared of going to Hell. Fire was a childhood phobia of mine. There was always an unnamable fear, an underlying anxiety that plagued my child's brain. I just wanted to be good and do everything right so I could get to Heaven. I walked around holding my little Bible, wearing my crocheted white shawl, Mary Jane shoes on my feet. I presented a pious little picture.

There was just one thing. It was my hair. My extra-thick mountain of luxurious hair. It was up in two ponytails all the time and they were huge. I always did and still do love big hair. Well, the ladies at church did not. It was suggested that my hair needed to be cut off.

One bright day after school, my mom said we were going somewhere, just me and her. "It's a surprise!" she said. I was excited because that wasn't a common event. Just me and my mom! Wow! We pulled up to a tropical looking building. She led me into a room with lots of funny chairs. I was led to sit in one and before I knew what was happening my beautiful ponytails were chopped off and lying on the floor. They did not ask me or anything. I was stunned as the stylist kept chopping at my head. When they spun the chair toward the mirror, I screamed. I could not stop sobbing. I felt betrayed, somehow, like they were trying to change me into a different person. It's as though I felt that symbolism, even as a child, and I was pissed! My hair looked like a stupid mushroom.

At church I got comments about how much better my hair looked and that now I looked like a "proper young lady." How I grew to hate that phrase! The mentalities of the denomination my family belonged to (Church of Christ in Christian Union) were fifty years behind the times! No, a hundred! For example, my cousin and I were racing with some kids outside. When it was my turn to race my cousin, I beat him. When I walked back to the house my grandma pulled my arm and just started slapping me, my butt, my face, wherever. I sobbed, "What did I do?" She said, "He's a boy! You let him win! You are getting too big for your britches!" Another time when I got straight A's, again, she said "It's not gonna matter anyway, 'cause you're a girl!"

The hatred of women by women was astounding to me. A preacher touched me inappropriately and the sentiment was "What did you to make him do that?" I was wearing one of those Spanish-style layered off-the-shoulder dresses and orange hoop earrings. She told me that women were to be "unadorned". When I took a bath that night, the dress and the earrings disappeared. I felt that they were all trying to crush my natural spirit. And thus, the mountain of rage was forming, forming.

One Sunday, I was laughing with another girl in the hallway after church, not even during the service or anything. The preacher, with a raised voice, said menacingly, "The devil's got you, little girl!" He advised the girl's mom not to let her around me. It felt like the whole church hated me. I was an outcast with no reason why.

My grandma advised me that I had "backslid" and should be ashamed. I was sent to "Jesus Camp," a place where strict gender roles were enforced and everyone within their gender were all expected to be the same (something I strongly bristle at today). We had to do a lot of chores and go to church three times a day. There was no privacy in the bathroom. I was not comfortable pooping in front of the other girls and I got constipated. The monitor would not let me go later during service, even though I begged. I pooped in my pants. No one found out, but it was humiliating. On the plus side, I would sneak off and go be in nature. I really knew by this time that something not right was going on here. These people were anti-life.

Home from camp I was not the same person. I already felt anger at the hypocrisy I had witnessed. Only nature and hard-rock music helped me feel that "Higher Power" feeling that I first felt during the beautiful hymns.

I was reaching puberty. In school, we learned briefly about Sigmund Freud. I kept independently reading about him. I was interested in dreams. I eventually came upon Jung's writings. I devoured them, even though I was so young. There was something I was trying to understand, the mystical nature of life.

I had spiritual experiences listening to "Holy Diver" by Ronnie James Dio. I'm still a huge fan. That sounds cute and laughable, but I had discovered something numinous. A world of fantasy, sword and sorcery and that I had been before.

After acting out and rebelling for a while, my whole life changed. Karen came into my life. She was the mother of my best friend Steve from school. He invited me to go to her house out in the country for a gathering. He said, "You will love my mom. Everybody does. She's weird, like you." I knew that was a compliment because even then, I dressed and acted according to my own nature more than your average 15 year old. I got both admiration and consternation for it.

Karen's house was so cool! A whole wall by the kitchen was just jars and jars of herbs and things. Her house smelled so good! When we were introduced I felt like I knew her already. I just loved her immediately! She was a jolly sort of person with long, curly silver hair. Cool jewelry and stones adorned her person.

She seemed to find me familiar, too. She patiently answered all my questions about this herb and that. She took us down to the basement that was in the side of a hill so there was a patio just outside it. When she flipped on the light I was wowed. She ran an herb shop out of her "basement". The full moon shone right into the room.

Out of the blue, I said, "I want to be a witch". She smiled and said, "You already are!" She nurtured my curiosity about spiritual things. I began working in her shop, and did so for many years. She gifted me with The Herbal Tarot and I began learning Wicca from her, mostly by osmosis or example, but she gave me books and had so many invaluable conversations with me. I met other witches through her. I can honestly say she saved my life. She got annoyed when I called her my teacher, though. She said she was a student. I get that now.

My first experience with the Goddess that was more than just inspiration came during a rough patch in my teens. One bad thing after another had happened and I was outside in nature, crying my eyes out. "Just show me your beauty!" I cried to the full moon. Suddenly, the tree seemed to curl around the moon, like it was her hand, holding a giant pearl. Her face appeared in the trees and her eyes gazed at me and passed through me. The leaves became her hair. Words don't do it justice. I get goose bumps writing about it even after all these years.

I was fortunate to meet some beautiful like-minded souls and we had a cute little coven for many years until we moved away or apart. I have been a solitary witch for the most part since then. I have recently joined the Correllian Tradition. I like them and they are progressive. I am working on my first degree.

I am the proud mother of my transgender son. Due to my many unpleasant experiences with religion, of which these stories are just a drop in the bucket, I am keenly aware of how important human rights are. Seeing people as "other" is a slippery slope, indeed.

In that spirit, I will share an experience I had with Jesus. I was going through my Saturn return. A real "dark night of the soul" was upon me. I was at the end of my rope. Automatically, I said "Jesus help me!" He appeared and lifted me off my feet. I was hanging there for a minute. He looked amused and set me down. He was too cool to have been down with that toxic Christianity that was all I knew. I tried to reach him years later but his phone must have been busy. I suggest those who are drawn to Christianity to seek that guy out. He likes us all to be a little bit different from each other, he told me. "Red and yellow, black and white, they are precious to his sight..."

Nicki Ojeda "Tatiara" was born in 1971. She has been Wiccan, Witch and Pagan since the age of 15. She was a Renaissance festival performer and is still a professional Tarot reader.

my path to the mother

By Leeanen Sidhe

PERHAPS SOME OF YOU MIGHT WONDER what turned me away from Christianity to Paganism. When I was a child I grew up in a rural area and was surrounded by the natural world. My father had also grown up in a rural place and he loved to plant and grow things. We had fruit trees and berry bushes and a vegetable garden. Wild animals could frequently be seen and I can remember watching the deer sparing for mates in the forest below our house. I remember in February going looking for fallen deer antlers and seeing wild hares, foxes, ravens and doves. The woods and rolling grasslands were my playgrounds.

When I was six years old a family friend and neighbor came to the house and told us we should to join her church. Mom had been brought up Catholic and preferred her old faith even though she hadn't been to church in many years. But the neighbor lady insisted and even brought her pastor to our home. He had us watch movies about why their church was so much better than the others. My father would make himself scarce during these visits and I often wished I had too. My mother finally relented and we (she and I) started going to this new church.

Both my mother and I became active in the church. There were some parts I enjoyed like the singing and the summer Bible school arts and crafts but there were some parts that I did not agree with. In the children's regular Bible study class I often had questions that no one could really answer. I remember being taught about how Eve angered God and destroyed paradise by accepting the apple from the serpent. My teacher told us it was then that all the animals turned on each other for food. She said, "Where once the lion lay down with lamb in peace the lion now would kill and eat the baby lamb."

I asked, "What did the lion eat before?" The teacher confidently replied that he ate grass. I asked, "If the lion ate grass then why did he have sharp teeth meant for eating meat?" She replied that his teeth were different before Eve sinned. Then I said, "I thought you told us that all the animals were made as they are now and that they didn't evolve like they tell us in regular school."

She was getting cross with me now and said, "That's right, evolution is a lie, the animals were always as God made them, as we see them today." I then replied, "But if the lions teeth changed after Eve sinned isn't that evolution?" She just reiterated that evolution was a lie and that God made all the creatures as they are and that is the truth. Confused I asked, "If evolution isn't real then how come they keep finding all those fossils in the ground?"

She finally said, "We who believe in God's word don't believe in evolution, we believe God created the earth and everything in it and that's what He wants us to believe because His word is the truth." She then dismissed the class to go out and play but held me aside and told me that what I learn in public school is not acceptable to talk about in Bible school and admonished me not to bring up such subjects again. I was about nine years old then but it seemed wrong to me that I should not be allowed to discuss what I learned in public school in church. After all, weren't we here to learn the answers? I quickly figured out that the correct answers in school were very different as to what was correct in church.

That led me to learn all I could about the world from different points of view. What it all came down to was that what the church had to say about the world was not consistent with what I had observed in nature. I remember thinking that what the church and the Bible said all seemed made up to me, like fairy tales in children's books.

When I was twelve, I asked my father why he never went to church with my mother and me. He answered that his mother had taken him and his brothers and sisters to church every Sunday, but he didn't really seem to think that any of what the preacher or the Bible talked about made any sense. He said that the only words of worth in the Bible were the 10 Commandments and the Golden Rule and the rest was just horse hooey. My father had never expressed his opinions about religion before that and never has since then, either. He and I rarely saw eye-to-eye on things, especially after I became an adult, but this was one of the few things we agreed upon.

By the time I was fourteen I no longer wanted to go to church and I told my mother so. I thought she would scold me and try to force me to go as my mother was usually very strict and demanding. But she didn't. She told me that her mother had changed religions when she was a young girl and after being brought up Catholic she was forced to leave that faith behind and join the new faith her mother had chosen. That religion was the same one practiced in the church she and I had been part of all those years, the same church that my grandmother and the rest of her side of the family all belonged to. I then understood that the reason my mother had agreed to join the church in the first place was to please my grandmother and get back in her good graces. She and her mother had had a big fight over it long ago ending with my grandmother giving my mother an ultimatum, that she either join the church or leave home. My mother chose the latter. She told me that she always had resented her mother doing that and that she didn't want to force a religious faith on me that I didn't believe in. I was stunned. She added that religion is something that you should come to willingly, that it means nothing if you don't believe in it. A few years after I stopped going to church, she stopped also.

It would be years later when I came to believe in Paganism. After leaving the church I just continued to observe nature and form my own beliefs about what I thought God was. I talked to many people of many different faiths and read many books, too. But the epiphany came when I wrote a paper for a college English assignment in which I was to pick one of the subjects given and in my own words describe it. I was the only one in class who chose the topic of God. My paper impressed the class and the professor and she told me that what I had to say sounded much like the belief in "animism." I was curious so I checked out books in the library on anything I found. The internet was not really in existence back then so information was scarce. But what I did find lead me to an ancient belief system that touched my heart and soul. It was so much like what I believed already and it prompted me to learn more.

A few years later, I became sick with a persistent and crippling illness. Traditional medicine wasn't helping and I was told that there was nothing that could be done. While the illness wouldn't kill me the damage that had been done to my immune system and other systems in my body seemed irreversible and that I would just have to get used to living my life as being handicapped. I refused to accept their diagnosis and searched for alternative healing methods. I found books written on meditational healing and herbal medicine. My search also led me to find more information on Goddess worship and Paganism with regards to healing through a return to nature and the gifts She had given us in herbs and roots with medicinal properties. It took me three years of meditational healing and herbal medicine but at last the illness that I was told was incurable finally left me. I was no longer disabled and could return to an active life.

Soon after my recovery I celebrated with a long walk in the woods, something I had not done in many years. That next morning, early, when it was still dark, I awoke and felt a feeling wash over me, warm and gentle and comforting as a mother's touch. Indeed, there seemed to be a feminine presence there with me. In my mind I saw a vision of a special gift of herbs and flowers lain on my pillow and though the room was dark, these things seemed to glow with a blue light. I knew I was not dreaming and I knew that in "reality" these things were not really there, yet this sending was as clear as if it were real. The feeling that came to me then was one of welcome and peace and joy.

When I needed Her, She was there to show me the answer that not only cured me of my illness but brought a peace and understanding to my soul that Christianity had never brought me. Afterwards I dedicated three more years of my life to study and worship of the Goddess, living as close to a monastic life as I could, only going to school and work. That time gave me a very solid spiritual foundation that has been unshakable. Ever since then the Goddess has been there to guide me whenever there was difficulty or uncertainty in my life. It was only when I didn't follow Her guidance that I would get into trouble and I wouldn't get out of it again until I stopped being stubborn and listened to what my Goddess given instincts were telling me.

I am devout in my faith and I am not ashamed of it, yet I do tend to keep it secret for fear revealing it may bring harm to me or to the people I care about. I think it is a shame I cannot be more open about it and I am trying to help change that by shedding light on some of the falsehoods that continue to be perpetuated about my chosen faith. My faith is known as the faith without converts. I am not here to say that my faith is the only right faith but I am here to say is that it is the faith that is right for me. I and others who follow the same path should be allowed to do so without persecution and without demonizing of our faith by those who really know nothing about it but think they do.

In my opinion, religion and spiritual belief is a very intimate and personal thing. What you experience during times of meditation or prayer is between you and your chosen deity. Your experiences should have meaning that is special to you, that touches you and causes you to see things in way you have not seen them before. It should enlighten you and bring joy to your heart. It should inspire you to act out of kindness, move confidently through the world and give your best effort to everything you choose to take on. It should cause you to feel the sacredness in and respect for all things from the highest mountain to the tiniest insect. It should give you comfort when you fall, courage when you fear, humility when you fail and dignity when faced with those who belittle you. All this your faith should bring you without the need to convert, condemn or harm anyone or anything else.

I firmly believe that The Truth we so desperately seek cannot be found anywhere else except within the tangible things that came to us directly from the hand of our Creator, and that is the study and observation of the Earth and the Universe and all the life within it.

I leave you with this question: Is it not time for all people of all faiths and beliefs, even those of non-belief, to put aside our age-old differences, to respect and accept our differences and to finally notice just how similar we all are to each other?

Peace comes only through understanding.

Leeanen Sidhe has been an eclectic Wiccan for 30 years. She was part of a coven for 7 years. She was a member the Sonoma County Pagan Network for 16 years serving on its board of directors for much of that time. She also has participated in and facilitated public rituals and has been recognized as a Wiccan Priestess in her community. She is now a solitary practitioner and lives in the San Francisco Bay Area with her husband.

the path of spiritual beauty

By Cheryl Sherman

MY MOM AND I WENT TO PRESBYTER-
ian and Lutheran Churches on Christmas and
Easter. We seldom went otherwise except
when we were at my grandparents' house.

When I was fifteen, to escape an abusive
stepfather, I went to a neighborhood church where there was a thriv-
ing music program. Some of my school friends attended. I accepted
Jesus and was 'born again,' enjoying music as a way of worship and
self-expression of my love for God. It was a good experience for
about twenty years.

Wanting to delve deeper into who God was, in my late thirties I
got a Theology and Ministerial Degree. Upon graduation, even with
my two degrees I wasn't taken seriously by the church I was attending, by friends, etc. It was very painful.

I served in the nursery, baby-sat and taught young children Bible
classes using color book Bible pages. I did it cheerfully, but became
disheartened over the continued lack of opportunity to teach teenagers and adults.

I was in my 40s when I left the programming of the Christian
church. It was hard to unplug myself from the doctrine of hell, damnation and Jesus horrid blood sacrifice. Because of my theology degree, I had learned of the many sacred views around the world. I
started looking into them. Paganism began to resonate with me.
There was a God and Goddess—family.

After a divorce, I remarried, moved to a different state where my
mother passed. She had been my best friend. I was devastated.

I joined the Grey School of Wizardry and enjoyed studying
about magickal traditions. A few other women and I started a small
circle, doing celebrations and rituals for several years. We each
wrote and hosted (being Priestess) the ritual/celebration. But life got
busy and our group slowly disbanded. During that time, I began il-
lustrating and writing YA novels which involved tons of research. I

studied star-seeds, Delores Cannon, *Life between Lives* and saw UFO craft at our ranch in AZ and in CA at Contact in the Desert.

Being an avid reader, I studied *The Emerald Tablets*, *The Law of One*, the *Book of Enoch*, and *The Urantia Papers,* among other books. I found a deep connection with our Universal Creator. I discovered that God the Father was not the angry tribal God of the Old Testament. The man-made idea of Jesus death was because of man's cruelty not something God needed so that he might love his so-called, 'born-in-sin' children.

I live about an hour from most areas, so I don't get off the ranch much. I work with my horses, garden, study, research, write and illustrate my novels that have won nine awards. My spirituality continues to grow and has become an inner journey not an outer one. I don't need to go back to church where the doctrine is flawed. Looking back, I know every part of my spiritual journey was necessary. I had to learn, to experience and not be afraid to explore spiritually, wherever that took me. I take spirituality classes and continue my daily research.

We all have a spark of the One Source and Center who is the great Creator within us. Gregg Braden's book, *The God Code,* talks of the 'God-Eternal-Within-The-Body' DNA code. The spark within will lead us back to the One who loves our soul, who gave us personality and God-consciousness. We all start on our own hero's journey in this life. Being spiritual, not fearful, keeping our hearts and minds open to the loving Creator is our foremost assignment while here on this planet. After this material life, if we so desire, we will have an eternity to discover the ultimate and wondrous truth, beauty and goodness of Deity.

Living on a ranch with long horn cattle and training horses keeps me busy. As the author of Ocean Depth A Darkness novel 1, Ocean Depths A Time novel 2, Ocean Depths A Life novel 3 *I've had a blast creating and continuing the story plot of gods and goddesses interacting with us on our planet. The novels have won nine awards, three per book. I'm so grateful for the kudos and am working on novel 4,* Ocean Depths A Dream. *I also enjoy creating the illustrations of my characters in water color for each of the novels and their covers. Spirituality is a process, and I'm thrilled to be on a path of continuing enlightenment!*

JOURNEY OF A BELIEVER

By Thomas Clare Lee, Jr.

I was raised in the Seventh-Day Adventist church. It was fine as a child; my family was devout without being overly devout. My father had gone to college to be a pastor and got his bachelor's degree in theology, though he never became a pastor. My parents separated when I was ten and were divorced by the time I was twelve. My father had left the church at this point, but my mother still attended and became a Deaconess, eventually being the Head Deaconess for the Eugene, Oregon church. She was also heavily involved with the youth group Pathfinders, where she was a Master Guide and Director. Due to this, my sister and I were also heavily involved.

I was baptized when I was thirteen but even after going through the classes I truly did not understand what it meant. I spent two years at the church school supported by the church. Due to the divorce and stress and other things, I started to question things. When I was seventeen, I joined the US Army where I went into combat arms, even though Seventh Day Adventist was listed as a religion for the basis of being a conscientious objector. This caused me some struggles mentally and spiritually.

During this period, I completed the requirements to become a Pathfinder Master Guide. I also got married to my first wife who was also a Seventh Day Adventist.

After getting out of the Army in 1990, I became involved in the Church by becoming an ordained Deacon, Young Adult leader and youth group leader along with working in Pathfinders. I also spent time as a Literature Evangelist and Bible study leader. I began to have doubts as I suffered physical and mental abuse at the hands of my first wife. It finally became too much and I divorced after twelve years. The pastor of the church in Lebanon, Oregon where we lived at the time, tried to get me excommunicated from the church. I told him off and told the church conference for Oregon to remove me from the membership books.

I remarried and struggled to find my spiritual path. Due to my studies and my time spent in the church, I realized that Christianity was no longer the path for me. Christianity was too full of hypocrisy, along with misinterpretation of the Bible to support each group's goals and desires. During this time of searching, I became friends with a group who were Pagans following the Celtic path. My friend was a Druid, having completed training. I began to learn about astral travel and began to really investigate other religions. I also had resumed my martial arts journey at this time.

During this time of exploration and learning, I became excited about Taoism, Zen, Buddhism and Hinduism. I also felt myself pulled to the Norse tradition. I became an ordained Dudeist Priest in 2012 and really settled into a belief in Mother Gaia. My family has mostly been okay with my changes, though my mother still struggles as she still feels she is a Christian.

My journey lately has mainly been a solo one, I belong to groups on Facebook and have attended several events in the Portland/Vancouver area. I have not found a group to really attach myself to, but I am looking. I know when it is time, Gaia will guide me to where I need to be.

I can honestly say that I no longer believe that Jesus was or is the Son of God. I also do not accept the current Christian version of God because most Christians do not actually live like Christ. It is also because Christianity is a patriarchal system that is contrary to history and life, a system that subjugates women and family.

What I would like to convey to current Christians and clergy is to really look at the history of the Bible and society. To look at how it has changed due to man's decisions with no actual reflection of what the Bible says or the history of when the Bible was written. The truth is not hard to find, and if you will really open yourself to the world and the universe you will find the path.

Thomas Clare Lee Jr., born July 22, 1966. 2ⁿᵈ Degree Black Belt. Advanced Instructor Bram Frank's Modular Knife System. Retired 100% Disabled Veteran.

part iii:

appendix

Goodbye Jesus,
I've gone Home
to Mother

a.
why pagans can't be converted to christianity, in the words of pagans themselves

Luke 14:25-26. *Large crowds were traveling with Jesus, and turning to them, He said, "If anyone comes to me and does not hate father and mother, wife and children, brothers and sisters — yes, even their own life — such a person cannot be my disciple."*

WIZARD OF ID | *Brant Parker*

© 2021. Reprinted by permission of John Hart Studios Inc. and Creators Syndicate, Inc.

've seen a lot of books and other writings put out by Christian groups advising their missionaries and proselytutes on how to evangelize and convert us Pagans to Christianity. I see that as a hopeless cause, since most of us who were not actually raised Pagan (as many are these days…) came originally from Christian or Jewish backgrounds, which we left deliberately—not out of ignorance. And we have no desire to go back. After all, that's what this book is all about!

As I was gathering essays for this compendium, it occurred to me to put out a note on Facebook asking my FB friends to submit

their own reasons "Why Pagans can't be converted to Christianity."
I got more than 200 responses! Here are some of the best. ~ OZ

Grieg Pedersen: I just cite Hebrews 6:4-6 and send them on their
way: *"For it is impossible for those who were once enlightened, and
have tasted of the heavenly gift, and were made partakers of the
Holy Ghost, and have tasted the good word of God, and the powers
of the world to come, if they shall fall away, to renew them again
unto repentance."*

I had problems with the many internal and real-world contradictions in Christian churches. Christians say that there is only one
God, that Jesus was God, and the only the Father (not even the Son)
knows the time of His return. How's that again?

Matthew Lee Martin: I was raised a southern Baptist until I turned
13. I was even baptized. I didn't feel the Holy Spirit enter me like
they said it would. I went through a "dark night of the soul" and
woke up embracing my family's original [Irish Pagan] faith from
before St Patrick arrived. I think most of us who learned about our
ancestors and our origins have chosen to continue on in our forefa-
thers' and mothers' footsteps.

My biggest thing was "thou shalt not have any other Gods before
me." I always thought that means there *are* others.

I never felt guilt about leaving Christianity. It felt natural when
I realized it wasn't for me.

Hell never made sense to me, and the whole god hates homosex-
uals thing really irked me. If God is love, then God couldn't have
made hell a permanent place nor could God hate anyone for any reason; that's what gets me Christians preach about unconditional love,
yet to be admitted into heaven you have to meet a condition.

Amy Willmore-Cochran: I was also once Christian, but never felt
like it was right for me. It's all those "thou shalt not's" that I have
issue with. I feel like I know what's right and wrong in my heart and
can live accordingly.

Dara Bowers: Christianity has very little to do with Jesus or what
he taught. Most of what is currently Christianity is about the Without

rather than going Within to the Source to Divinity Within. I go to the Gods, the Lord and Lady within. As Within, so Without, As Above, so Below.

Ute Hütten: Christianity, like many religions, is based on fear. The fear of the unknown, offering comfort in answers. But one needs to learn to trust life, to live in the here and now. I stopped believing in the deity when I was about 8 years old. I didn't understand the discrepancy between the loving god they told us about, and on the other hand that we should fear him and the hardship he could bestow on us.

Paul E. Clinco: The fact is, most people don't want to be "converted;" most people prefer to evolve their own spiritual/religious path(s) without the intrusive badgering.

I'm considerably lucky that I was raised without any organized religion whatsoever, and discovered for myself how vicious ordinary people, acting as "Christians," can be. That was a long time before I discovered the contemporary Pagan subculture. The poetry of the ancient tales touched me in a way that the tales of the late Stone Age and early Bronze Age cultures in the Bible never did.

What the Pagan world has to offer is much more valuable than anything which modern Christianity has, especially complete spiritual and intellectual liberty and a total lack of dogma.

Resilient Tietan: I left because the path chose me. This path is about the mastery of self and understanding the self in the elementals and universe, not worshiping a state-sponsored death cult.

Maureen Aisling Duffy-Boose: In a nutshell, Pagans do not believe that man is "fallen" and do not believe there is anything from which we must be "saved." This world is not "outer darkness," but instead is the realm of flesh where we are sourced and from which we must contact Spirit.

Christianity is all about looking somewhere other than where one is, and leaving the present behind in search of an ineffable future exaltation. Pagans know the value and sacredness of the NOW, and focus on the immanent manifestations of the sacredness of this moment. We don't need a Savior, and we do need to be here now.

I think Gandhi had it right, and his comment answers the question for me: "I like your Christ, I do not like your Christians. Your Christians are so unlike your Christ."

Lisa Peschel-Hoerter: I had some Pagan friends tell some Jehovah's Witnesses "Why would I want to worship your dead god? My gods are alive."

I think Jesus would be a Pagan. My first problem with the Bible is the Old Testament. Shouldn't even be in there. When Christ came and preached the New Testament, it was all about love and tolerance and helping out the less fortunate. All that fire and brimstone crap the fundamentalists spew is NOT the words of Jesus. Jesus preached the New Testament because he disavowed the Old Testament. He was showing people a new way of freedom and thinking. Christ is pretty damn cool, actually. It's Christianity that's fucked up.

Summer-Jezebel Raine: Once we have heard the voice of our mother and she has embraced us and we have found truth, no "his"-story can be sold to us again. They are "believers;" we are "knowers."

Sue Wolfsong: My divine connections 'speak' directly to me, not through an intermediary who sees things differently than I do and can cause me to be slavishly following human directives rather than those of divinity. As a priestess, it's not my job to tell people what to do, but to help them open themselves to their own awakening. This freedom is what we enjoy as Pagans. We're responsible for our own actions and have to answer accordingly. We need no human to intervene imposing the concept of guilt, fear and sin upon our souls that are one with everything.

Marilyn Ascione Roberts: I was raised in the Roman Catholic church. About ten years ago I decided it was too discriminatory to women.

Lisa Kay Hollingsworth: Anyone can be converted to anything if their state of mind is such that something is not working for them and there is no support. Those who were not raised in the Craft came to it because of bad experiences, dogma, or because they felt disconnected from Nature.

I believe in change and balance as a lot of us do. When we are restricted we say uh, nope, that doesn't sound right to me. Your soul will know it.

I did *think* about going to a church and did for awhile, to fit in, to have a break from persecutions, but the Gods could only take so much of that and I had no peace until I was true to my beliefs and my Gods.

Ian Corrigan: For me, polytheism is just plainly more logical and in better conformity with Nature as I perceive it than is monotheism.

Sede Ling: Neo-Paganism is inclusive whereas Christianity seems largely exclusive. One may follow one or many Christs in Neo-Paganism and pursue their wisdom freely, whereas in Christianity one will typically be restricted to a defined set of teachings. I openly follow Jesus Christ as (among other things) the greatest hippie magi of all time. A step toward the Christian church would really be a step backwards for me.

Victoria Rouch: I can't be converted because I came to where I am after a childhood of knowing that Christianity was not the path for me. I've already been converted away from a Christian culture that I could not identify with and to a Pagan culture that allows me to grow and reach out to others with tolerance and patience.

Michael Ryan: The reason that I think Pagans (true, committed to their paths Pagans) would never convert to Christianity is that we have an imminent connection to our Deities every day and night. Also our religion makes sense to us because it's a personal path. By and large, most of us walk our own path and consider it the height of arrogance to try and ram it down the throat of some poor, unsuspecting Joe Average. All we can do is set a good example and maybe they will catch on and leave us alone.

Anastasia Aldridge: I've come to the conclusion that Pagans are hard to convert to Christianity because Paganism is a religion of THIS life and enjoying life now, Christianity is a NEXT life religion that suggests abstaining from human desires in hopes for a better afterlife. Most people would like to enjoy their life and therefore look to a religion that celebrates humanity instead of demonizing it.

Leo Sapphire: I never once entered any church that didn't have a pall of darkness hanging over it and within it. Desperate people were trying constantly to drive out the Darkness not realizing they brought it with them.

When I became Pagan, the light of Life and Love filled me and I have never looked back. I walk in their Love and Power every day and I do not need a preacher or his book to tell me that my God/dess is real.

Starwind Evensong: Most of us came from a Christian background. But for me, the Earth was always more special; it had more lessons to teach and impacted my life in far more ways than some distant God-figure. As I grew older I realized the Biblical stories were myth much like other mythologies. Divinity is in us and is all around us. It is not separate, but part of us all.

I could never go back to the Christianity of today, which from my perspective, is completely misinterpreted. The greatest lesson of the Christ is love, and love is not exhibited by many of his followers.

Malachite Storm: A Pagan would have to rewrite everything they believe in to be converted, which to me is almost impossible. I don't like broccoli, and you can't make me like it because you force it down my throat, or threaten me because in the end, I will still dislike it. If it's not in you, then it's not. Leave it be. Do what thou Wilt.

Morwen Two-Feathers: There's another aspect of Paganism that I think is important, and that comes into play when I discuss religion/theology with Christian friends and family. It's not simply about embracing "the gods" as symbols or metaphors for aspects of being human, there's the element of recognizing that the Earth (and everything on it, including animals, water, rocks, etc.) is SACRED. This sense of the sacred does not require rejecting science, but it is not fully explained by science either. It's no more "provable" than the Christian theology, but it leads to quite different (and in my view clearly superior) outcomes in terms of behavior and choices and values. Judaism, on the other hand, has a "reconstructionist" thread within it that is embracing shamanism, and honoring the way the natural cycles of the Earth has always been the basis for Jewish life and celebration. That's why I haven't felt a need to reject my Jewishness in order to be Pagan, as my formerly Christian friends have.

Deborah Hall: I respect everyone's belief in their gods but I do not believe in a "god" myself. My Source is the energy of the universe itself and my religion revolves around reverence for everything created from that energy, which of course is everything.

Jennifer Lawrence: I left Catholicism because of very specific problems and issues within that faith; Paganism has none of those problems (it has a set of problems of its own, but none of them involve treating women and GLBT people like 2nd class citizens, blaming others for things they didn't do, or deliberately covering up decades -- or more -- of child abuse). There is no chance I'd go back to that faith, no matter how wonderful some of its ideals are.

Marilyn Kellogg: I was raised Pagan, even though I'm sure my parents didn't know that is what they were doing (I wish they were still here with me so I could talk to them about it). Tried the "church thing", but it's not for me. Why should I spend money on expensive clothes, to go to a building to try to impress others and pay someone to preach to me, when every time I look or go outdoors, I AM in church.

Virginia Anderson: My personal path to and in Paganism has involved finding deeper understanding of myself and Nature. It is really a path of self-exploration as opposed to Christianity which involves being told what to believe.

Angela Marra-Sudano: I was baptized and raised in the Catholic faith, but one of my husband's family members became a [Jehovah's Witness]. A few of her friends have tried to convert me, claiming that Catholicism is a lie and that Christ wasn't born in December (insert gasp here). So I guess it's not just Pagans that more fundamentalist Christian groups are trying to "convert." Apparently I'm not Christian enough for the Jehovah's Witnesses, or the Born

Agains, or the Baptists... I wonder what would happen if I told them about my involvement with Golden Dawn groups or my interest in Strega. If you are pursuing your True Will (a term I borrow from Thelema but really applies well to all magickal paths) then all roads lead to Rome. When I do attend Church (which is probably a few times per year) I pretty much hear "wawawawa" like the Charlie Brown teacher in the background while I concentrate on connecting to the energy. I sit there looking at the two podiums, one marked with Alpha and the other with Omega. I look at the two pillars in the North and South with the crucifix in the middle and realize that I'm looking at a Qabalistic Tree of Life.

Holly Hutter Diaz: My mother was a "free thinking" Christian and my father was more of an agnostic. My mother professed she was Christian and yet studied astrology and palmistry and even Tarot, which she was very good at. Even though she encouraged us to try Christianity while we were young, I never connected with it. I felt there was much more to spirituality. I had my first out of body experience when I was 8, heard and felt certain entities calling to me, could tell when something was wrong with family members that were hundreds of miles away, and then, when I was about 12, I heard a voice say "You are now on the right path, follow me." Ever since, it has not led me astray and has always been there for me spiritually. I cannot say it is a Goddess or God or something else, but I have always felt that it was both.

Many of my abilities and "supernatural" instincts have come from my mother's side of the family. When I was about 17, she told me of how she, her grandmother, great aunt, and great-great grandmother had similar abilities. One was even a Shaman of a Sioux Indian tribe, [on] her grandfather's side of the family. Her father was from Norway and after looking through his heritage and history, I felt a calling to some of the Asatru pantheon. There is no way that I would go back to a belief with so many hypocrites who have used the stories of our ancient deities to form a belief of their own.

Isis Rose: As a ChristoPagan (no not a "blended" religious faith and not an oxymoron), I've had my beliefs all my life. I was raised with them. I just didn't learn that there was such a thing as ChristoPaganism until I learned about Paganism. But proselytizing is immoral.

Look what it did to the Irish, the Scots, the Welsh and the Native Americans.

Seth Tyrssen: We do not need intermediaries to "talk to God" for us, and we see the holy life-essence in all things, not just in egocentric humans. The last time the local Baptists came around to convert me, they were reduced to sputtering "you're wrong, you're wrong" when they couldn't counter my arguments, and they never returned.

Laine Wrae Thornton: "I once was blind and now can see..." I cannot accept the Christian faith as it has evolved. Jesus never meant it to be what it has become! We take what feels right from many sources (for there is a grain of truth in all paths) and discard that which does not. To be slightly geeky: "The sleeper has awakened!" There is a revolution of the mind and soul taking place in the Universe and we are the center of the whirlwind.

Avens O'Brien: I was raised Neo-Pagan. Wiccan father, Druid mother. Both clergy. But I got a solid education of Abrahamic religions from college, family friends and grandparents. I respect Christianity -- but I couldn't be converted.

You see, I'm a solid polytheist. I don't reject the existence of Jehovah, Elohim, Allah, Jesus, whomever -- just as I don't reject the existence of Shiva, Vishnu, Ganesha, Zeus, Hera, Ra, Sekmet, etc. I was raised with respect to my Celtic and Norse ancestry, so the deities I actively honor are those of my Celtic and Norse ancestors. They are the ones who called me, formed my worldview and answer my prayers.

Christianity tends to be hostile towards my polytheism. Deuteronomy mentions God being a "jealous God", who wishes no other Gods before him. Alas -- that's just not possible for me.

Mark Colwell: Paganism is Love and Wonder unbridled and free. The most effective weapon Christians can wield is fear: fear of exclusion, fear of persecution, fear of burning in a fiery hell. Paganism holds a strong advantage because Love is more powerful than Fear and wonder more attractive than walls no matter how beautiful those walls might be. We are wild and we are free, what use do we have for the bridle of organized religion?

Debbie Young-Foley: Christianity just simply does not fit into my soul. I am of the Universe.

Sara West: Many people who are Pagan can't be converted to Christianity because a lot of us came from monotheistic beliefs before we found the Goddess. We are well-acquainted with the Christian faith and have found peace with what we believe now. Not to say Christianity is bad, just that it doesn't fit all needs for all folk.

Lezlie Kinyon: Because "converted" is an either/or monotheistic/Abrahamist notion and once you drop that idea, the world opens into infinite possibility.

Dorothy Litch: I was raised a Catholic and it took me years to shed the guilt and anxiety ! I could Never go back to that, after finding such harmony.

Priest Christopher Well you cannot make people believe something that does not make sense to them or that they do not want to follow. You can't even convince a particular Pagan to become another type of Pagan if their current path suits them best. Also, many Pagans came from Christianity, so clearly they didn't find what they were looking for there and found more in Paganism, so why would they go back to Christianity?

Faith Hamilton: Pagans cannot be converted to Christianity because they have taken upon themselves to study and read all that is historically biblical and found that there are too many questions that remain. Their natural curiosity for the unknown has compelled them to seek further. Going back to Christianity now with heads so full of so many things would be next to impossible, somewhat like trying to cram a whole loaf of bread in to a toaster at once and expecting everything to operate smoothly.

Joan Medina: Because I see the sacred and divine in the glory of the sunrise and the mystery of the sunset as well as in the beauty of the moon as it crosses the sky; I hear it whispered on the wind and along the path of the creepy crawlers, in the laughter of two-footed companions, in the thundering hoofbeat of my four-footed relations, and in the rush of flight as well as the peaceful soaring of my winged brothers and sisters; I taste it on the rain that falls from the sky and from the waters that flow from the rivers and oceans; I smell it from the blooming flowers of spring and on the snow-covered evergreens of winter, and I feel it beneath my feet through the heartbeat of the Earth that is my constant pulsing companion. I don't need a book written by men or the walls of a building around me or the presence of others to give credence to the holy presence of The Mother that is all around me. My connection to the sacred and divine does not require permission or precedence of any institution or other person.

I don't see how it would be possible to convert me since my spirituality comes from a place of respect for others (inclusive of all beings -- animals and plants as well as sea, sky and stone) and a sense of interconnection and love rather than fear and reprisal. I would rather dance under the full moon of night or bright sun of day and glory in the beauty and love that I continually find around me than embrace the fear-mongering of the Christian religion.

Pagans care not to convert for the idea of possible afterlife ecstasy in the Christian's heaven, because they already experience ecstasy and heaven here in this lifetime on earth, perhaps in quietly communing with ancient trees in the forest, or in feeling small yet connected while standing underneath a glorious blue expanse of sky, or maybe in dancing around a fire to the pounding rhythms of the drum circle while the stars in THESE heavens shine upon them.

Sam Bennett: It occurs to me that none of the children I know who were raised Pagan have become Christians. Many took a different path than that of their parents, some are even agnostic/atheist, but I can't think of a monotheist in the bunch.

A.C. Fisher Aldag: Let me precede this statement by saying most Christians are fairly nice people. However, I don't wanna go to heaven, I want to come back here. I live in the most beautiful place on Earth, and the idea of floating around in the clouds for all eternity is repugnant.

The inequality between the sexes is untenable. It comes from belief in only male deities. I believe that the Gods are my ancestors, not some ephemeral, omniscient being(s). I believe that the Earth is sacred, not base or profane; I don't think we should give up "Earthly Ways" but honor them. Sexuality, likewise, is sacred, all types of sexuality between consenting adults. Why would deity care to regulate that? Why would he/she give us sexual pleasure, if we weren't supposed to enjoy it? I view Christians as secretly being ashamed of their sexuality, as if it wasn't something to be honored. That is like Goddess giving us taste buds and chocolate, but we're not supposed to enjoy it. Lastly, the reason that I won't ever be converted to Christianity is their hatred and fear of magick. Again, a wonderful gift of the Gods that we are supposed to use and enjoy.

Jan Scott: I was raised in a non-religious home. I was not prevented from going to church but it was not encouraged either. I sought answers from my childhood, going to various sects, never quite finding anywhere I fit, or that could answer my questions, I could not accept the Bible as fact because it had been rewritten and translated so many times, and even as a child I knew that people included their own beliefs. I also knew that some of my "abilities" were unacceptable in the Christian Church. I can't go back to having to hide, and I won't. That is why I cannot be converted, besides, I ran out of cheeks to turn a long time ago!

Serendipity Niner: I was raised Christian. When I went through Confirmation, I read the Bible from cover to cover. The incoherence between books of the Bible led my faith collapse like Alice's pack of cards built into a fragile card house. I was atheist for a few years after that for lack of an alternative. Then I encountered friends in college who offered more coherent philosophies, and I became polytheistic agnostic. It only makes sense, given the tremendous diversity in the world, that divinity is likewise diverse. The whole world/universe exists in the image of the Divine (or perhaps the reverse). I am now an ADF [Ár nDraíocht Féin: A Druid Fellowship] Druid, because it is the one religion I have encountered that matches my current polytheistic experiences. I suppose on a political level, I am more UU [Unitarian Universalist] in that I think any religion that makes you a better person than you would be otherwise is worth following, regardless of whether your philosophy agrees with that of other humans.

Todd Kintz: I was raised in a Christian home, but in Wicca I have found a connection to Deities that I couldn't find anywhere else.

Johnny Angel: Christianity is a religion of death worship. Paganism loves and affirms life. Christianity is designed to keep you a slave. Paganism is designed to return you to your original place of freedom; without guilt or fear.

Kate Dennis: I was a Christian minister. As I child I was more impressed with the wonders of Nature than the stories in Sunday school about God. I thought immersing myself further into the Church would bring me a better understanding of the Divine. It did just the opposite: the dogma and elitism drove me out of the Church. My spirituality expanded which expanded my horizons in other areas of my life. I feel at peace where I am on my journey.

Kirsten Johnsen: Two quotes I enjoyed recently: "Never follow a dead guru" – Idris Shah

"If God made us in His image, we have more than reciprocated." (– unknown)

I would add another aspect to the conversation. It's the fear factor. To be converted, to clasp to a "One True Way" to the exclusion of all other ways of experiencing Deity, often requires a certain amount of fear of the unknown, fear of judgment, fear of darkness. Pagans, generally speaking, don't hold fear of the Shadow aspects of spiritual reality, the devouring Crone, the Reaper, the Callieach. Instead, we recognize and respect Her role in our lives and do our best to learn how to be more whole when it comes time to meet Her lessons. Knowing there is nothing to fear, even from the most terrifying of deity manifestations, liberates one from dualistic thinking.

Frances Campion: Our faith is a celebration of life and all of creation. We see joy in the Goddess's Mysteries as She turns the Wheel of Seasons; we revere all that is Divine from standing rock to singing bird. Christians mourn their faith with guilt and fear. We revere that by acknowledging that which is without and that which is within.

Mermyst Seastar: We generally are too tolerant of everyone's religion because the reflection of our own uniqueness does not mirror anyone else and can't be defined. Pagans, especially Texas Pagans, don't like to be told what to think, and none of us are exactly the same. Though our tenets are defined, we think for ourselves and take responsibility for our actions. Christians look to God for everything and ask God to take responsibility for their actions and forgive them. To tell someone who is tolerant and unique that they must fit in a cookie cutter mold, or they are unworthy of God(s)'s love does not make sense, nor is it reflected in Nature.

Sylveey Selu: Pagans can't be converted because of an inclination toward critical thinking. Some Christians aren't converted because they realize the absurdity of the Bible, but they remain Christian and are very spiritual, never harming anyone in thought or deed. After all, the taproot of Christianity is deep in the rich soil of Paganism.

Colette Giovanniello: Because I would not be here without the God AND Goddess; makes perfect sense to me!

Caerwyld OftheGoddess: At one time I followed Lord Yahweh. When I left to follow the Path of the Old Ones I had a long talk with Lord Yahweh about my choice. I made my choice and accepted the responsibility and consequences of that choice. THAT is why I cannot be "converted"!

Jim Lockhart: Immanuel Kant observed that most people are content with being spoon fed their religion and spiritual practices (and diet via TV commercials) mostly out of fear and spiritual ignorance or what he called 'immaturity'. I won't be that harsh however. Most Pagans I know are deathly allergic to being spoon fed anything, let alone their religion and spiritual practices and would be unlikely to convert to anything remotely resembling spoon-feeding.

Nahtrili Yorbizz: I met the Gods in the woods, the beach, the mountaintop. I am aware of the Great Goddess every day. They are alive and real. My spirituality broadened and eventually became a matter of developing relationship with Deity as manifested through Nature and the seasons. Later on my journey I was became aware of the Gods of the Temple and the Gods of the Tribe, but the real juice still comes from relationship with the Gods of the Grove. I realized that I was no longer able to be an Abrahamic monotheist (one who worships no other god) in good conscience. There is a lot of good in the Christianity I was raised in and because of that I would not be forsworn of my confirmation oaths. I wanted to remain a person of good conscience, so I continue to respect the practical, humanistic and positive message of most of Jesus's preaching, (setting aside the bits about how he came to bring a sword, set father against son, etc.). At any rate, I am at peace with the Christianity that is used by its adherents as a way toward human connection and personal spirit- I respect it but do not practice it. There is simply no reason for me to go back to it or to any of the monotheisms.

Christopher Blackwell: Basic Rules For Converting A Witch

So, you want to convert us to your religion. First, some basic information:

Understand that we love our religion perhaps even more than you love your religion.

We choose Witchcraft of our own free will. Nobody forced us into it. There were no threats of dire consequences if we didn't join. Nor are any threats keeping us in.

We can leave at any time should we feel the need to. We don't hold grudges against people who leave because we say at the start that this is not the religion for everyone.

Our religion does not teach against any other religion. Giving out hatred only brings hatred in return, and there is far too much of that as it is. We don't believe in adding to it.

Love unto all beings is one of our beliefs, though we may need to heal a bit before we fully understand that. But then, this is a lifetime path, and then some.

Please learn a bit about our religion. You don't want to appear ignorant as you try to tell us what in your opinion is wrong with it. Most attacks on our religion look so very foolish because it is obvious that the person never bothered to learn anything, and therefore is attacking some bit of their own imagination, or their religion's imagination, of what they think our religion is all about.

Learn about the limits of magic. It is not instantaneous, nor does it cause massive change. You have been watching too many Hollywood movies, if you think otherwise. My Goddess, if storm clouds always appeared overhead and all those flashes of light and smoke should show up every time we did magic, well, you would always know where we were and when we were doing it. Please, we are a little subtler than that.

Plus, even we know that we only have the right to work on our own lives. Anything we might do to anybody else would come crashing down on our heads three times over.

Plus, we have a life to live, too – jobs, families, hobbies – and we need time off to have some fun, perhaps see a movie or something. So where would we get the time for all the magic you think we're doing?

Sheesh, it takes time to get ready for a ceremony. Let me tell you, by the time we clean the place up, clean or shine our tools, lay the altar, do the ceremony and clean up afterwards, we have a few hours in, not even counting time to gather the necessary materials.

If your religion teaches that there is a religious war going on, it is a one-sided war at best. We are far too busy taking care of our own lives and those of our loved ones to have any time to play soldier, too.

I've been in a real war, and I can personally tell you that war is no fun, plus it takes up all of your time. The old '60s saying expresses my feelings: "What if they gave a war and nobody came?"

Oh, one more thing – Witchcraft teaches us to think for ourselves and take full responsibility for our own actions so we tend to refuse to let other people run our lives. So we won't convert to your religion until we are good and ready.

Personally, I think that you would have better luck elsewhere. We would be nothing but trouble in your religion anyway, since we don't follow orders very well, we tend to question everything, and we would probably break off and form our own church anyway.

Annette Davis: Proselytution should be illegal!

Kirsten Johnsen: Paganism is fun.

And that about sums it up.

B.
a timeline of
modern paganism

Decades of Witchcraft and Neo-Paganism

1900s-1920s   **60-year cultural renaissance: "The Golden Dawn."**
Magickal societies, arcane lodges, and esoteric fraternities. Creating liturgy for mystic rites & rituals.

1930s   Academics and folklorists spawn romantic writings and societies hearkening to old pagan ideals.

1940s   Foundational scholarly books of folklore and anthropology; earliest covens form.

1950s   British Tradition Witchcraft (BTW) becomes established and spreads, with considerable publicity.

1960s   **60-year cultural renaissance: "The New Age."**
Founding of various non-Wiccan groups; from 1967, all eventually claiming identity of "Pagan."

1970s   Pagan councils, alliances, and associations; early Pagan newsletters; Gaea Thesis (1970) unites Pagan community with common thealogy. First Pagan festivals and conventions.

1980s   Pagan Festivals proliferate; with home computers, explosive proliferation of Pagan publications.

1990s   Festivals become huge; major high-quality newsstand magazines; early internet, BBCs, etc.

2000s   Pagan businesses proliferate; newsstand magazines disappear or go digital; Paganism goes Internet. Pagan podcasts.

2010s   Pagan stores & festivals flourish; Facebook & YouTube; Pagan numbers increase exponentially into the millions; modern Paganism is recognized as the 2nd largest faith group in America, and the fastest-growing.

2020s   **60-year cultural renaissance: "The Awakening."**
In the great COVID pandemic, Pagan festivals go virtual and global via Zoom. Paganism becomes recognized as a major world religion, and a major player in Earth healing and restoration. New controversial issues threaten fragmentation.

The 20ᵗʰ Century

1938 Gleb Botkin (1900–1969), a Russian émigré to the US, founds The Church of Aphrodite in New York, worshipping in monotheistic fashion a female goddess who gave birth to the universe. One of Botkin's followers, W. Holman Keith, goes on to found the Neo-Dianic Faith in Los Angeles.

1940s Victor Anderson begins initiating others into what will become his Faerie (later "Feri") Witchcraft tradition. He later initiates Gwydion Pendderwen, Starhawk and others who become famous.

1946 Gerald Gardner joins Ancient Druid Order and its governing council. Gardner may have been initiated by Edith Woodford-Grimes ("Dafo") and founded his first coven this year.

1947 Gardner meets Aleister Crowley and becomes a member of the O.T.O. Crowley dies shortly thereafter.

Gardner begins writing his grimoire, *Ye Bok of Ye Arte Magickal*, which later becomes the *Gardnerian Book of Shadows*.

1948 Robert Graves publishes *The White Goddess*. His Triple Goddess later becomes a central motif in Wicca and feminist Witchcraft.

Gertrude Levy publishes *The Gate of Horn*, a study of archeological evidence for worship of a Mother Goddess in Neolithic Europe.

1949 Joseph Campbell publishes *The Hero With a Thousand Faces*. Campbell's Journey of the Hero monomyth is foundational for the Neo-Pagan mythos.

Gerald Gardner publishes *High Magic's Aid*, which describes a form of witchcraft resembling the witch religion of Murray's *God of the Witches*, worshiping a single male deity of fertility, with no mention of the Goddess.

1951 Gerald Gardner announces the existence of his Witch coven to the press. The modern revival of Witchcraft begins.

1953 Doreen Valiente is initiated by Gerald Gardner on Midsummer and becomes his High Priestess. Valiente works to revise Gardner's *Book of Shadows* as seen in his book *Witchcraft Today*.

1954 Gardner publishes *Witchcraft Today*, the first publication describing the purported origins of his Witchcraft revival.

1955 Jungian Erich Neumann publishes *The Great Mother*, tracing the Mother Goddess archetype from prehistoric times to the present.

1955 Esther Harding publishes *Women's Mysteries, Ancient and Modern*, a Jungian interpretation of the feminine principle in ancient myth.

1956 Following a mystical experience of the "Mysterious Feminine," Frederick Adams founds the Fellowship of Hesperides in Sierra Madre, CA, which later evolves into Feraferia. He emphasizes the

Kore (erotic/maiden) aspect of the Goddess trinity, celebrating an erotic union with Nature through an annual 9-point ritual cycle.

1957 Doreen Valiente splits with Gardner over his insistence on the priority of the God over the Goddess and his belief that the High Priestess must be young.

1958 Film *Bell Book & Candle* stars Kim Novak and Jack Lemon as cool modern-day Witches living in NYC's Greenwich Village.

1960 Victor & Cora Anderson found the Mahaelani coven, named after the Hawaiian word for the full moon.

1961 October. Robert A. Heinlein publishes *Stranger in a Strange Land.*

1962 Inspired by Heinlein's *Stranger in a Strange Land*, Westminster college students Tim Zell and Lance Christie share water on April 7 and found a water-brotherhood called Atl—antecedent to the Church of All Worlds.

Bewitched debuts on ABC-TV, introducing lovable Witch Samantha Stevens.

1963 The Reformed Druids of North America (RDNA) is founded at Carleton College, in Northfield, MN, as a protest against a requirement that students attend religious services.

Alexander Sanders is initiated by Pat Kopanski, and allowed to copy her *Book of Shadows.*

Ray Buckland is initiated by Lady Olwen into Gerald Gardner's coven in England.

Betty Friedan publishes *The Feminine Mystique.*

1964 The *Pentagram* is first published in the UK. The *Waxing Moon* is first published in the US by Joseph Wilson. These are the first Pagan periodicals.

Ray Buckland brings Gardnerian Wicca to US, establishing Long Island Coven and Museum of Witchcraft and initiating Americans into Gardnerian Witchcraft.

The Order of Bards, Ovates and Druids (OBOD) is founded by Ross Nichols after a schism within the Druid Order.

1965 Justine Glass publishes *Witchcraft, the Sixth Sense and Us.*

Martha Adler is initiated into Cincinnati coven. She is active in the Church of the Eternal Source and helps found the Pagan Way in 1970. Her coven later joins the Council of Themis and the Council of Earth Religions that succeeds it.

The Waxing Moon journal is founded by Joseph B. Wilson.

1966 Robert Graves' *The White Goddess* is republished by an American publisher in a revised and enlarged edition.

The Society for Creative Anachronism (SCA) is begun as a backyard party at the home of Diana Paxton in Berkley, CA. Marion Zimmer Bradley coins the name of the Society.

1967 Feraferia ("wild festival") is incorporated in southern CA by Fred
Adams as a continuation of his Fellowship of Hesperides.

New Reformed Orthodox Order of the Golden Dawn (NROOGD)
founded at San Francisco State University by Erif Thunen, Aiden
Kelly, Glenn Turner.

Julian Review published by Don Harrison, named after Julian, the
last Pagan Roman Emperor.

Atl and Church of All Worlds branch into two organizations; Atlan
Foundation remains underground, while CAW goes public. In St.
Louis, Tim Zell adopts label of "Pagan" for CAW and other Nature religion groups (Sept. 7), and files for incorporation of the
CAW as a Pagan church. Atl eventually incorporates as the Association for the Tree of Life (ATL), remaining under Lance's direction until his death at Samhain of 2010.

Rhuddlwm Gawr and Dynion Mwyn establish The Gathering of the
Tribes in Maryland.

1968 The Council of Themis is formed by Tim Zell of CAW and Fred
Adams of Feraferia. It is the first Pagan ecumenical Council.

CAW is formally chartered by the State of MO (March 4) and rents
temple, becoming the first state-recognized "Pagan" church. Tim
Zell begins publishing *Green Egg* (March 21), which becomes the
most important Neo-Pagan forum for many years. The publication
is instrumental in the formation of an emerging identity around
the word "Neo-Pagan" (later just "Pagan").

Delphic Fellowship is founded by Michael Kinghorn; the first seri-
ous attempt to bring together all the various modern Pagan groups
existing at that time. It is absorbed into the Council of Themis.

Sybil Leek publishes *Diary of a Witch*.

1969 Council of Themis is formed, named after the Greek Goddess of
harmony and councils.

Ordo Templi Orientis (OTO); first US chapter founded by Grady
McMurtry in Berkeley, CA.

Ordo Templi Astartes (OTA) founded by Carroll "Poke" Runyon;
incorporated in 1971.

Psychedelic Venus Church founded by Jefferson Fuck Poland, as a
successor to the Sexual Freedom League he had founded at San
Francisco State University several years before.

Donna Cole (Shultz) is initiated into a Gardnerian coven in England.
Shortly thereafter, Donna returns to Chicago where she and Herman Enderle form the first Pagan Way grove, eventually called
the Temple of the Pagan Way, which adopts Ed Fitch's new Pagan
Way materials.

Wiccan traditions begin to multiply over the next decade. Examples include the Mohsian/American Eclectic Traditional Wicca founded by Bill and Helen Mohs; the Georgian Tradition founded by George Patterson; the American Welsh Tradition founded by Ed Buczynski; Algard Wicca founded by Mary Nesnick; Blue Star Wicca founded by Frank Dufner; the Lothlorien tradition founded by Paul Beyer; and the Odyssean tradition founded by Richard and Tamarra James.

Ed Fitch, Joseph Wilson, Thomas Giles, Tony Kelly, and others begin circulating Fitch's "Outer Court Book of Shadows," initially intended as an introduction to Gardnerian Wicca, and his Pagan Way materials. The Pagan Way becomes a tradition in itself, with Pagan Way groves spreading across the country. In the UK, the movement is called the Pagan Movement, which splits into the Pagan Front in 1971, and is later renamed the Pagan Federation. On the US West Coast, Gwydion Pendderwen's Nemeton performs the same function, later becoming part of the Church of All Worlds.

1970 Witches International Craft Associates (WICA) founded by Louis Martello in New York.

First Earth Day, April 22. In St Louis, CAW is the only local church to participate.

The *Los Angeles Times* publishes an article entitled "Witchcraft Bubbles, Boils. Old Black Magic Casting New Spell" (5/5/70), which is one of the first of many positive articles about Witchcraft and Paganism to appear in newspapers across the country.

On July 10, the Church of All Worlds becomes the first Neo-Pagan group to be accorded 501(c)(3) religious non-profit status by the IRS. In contrast to Wicca or witchcraft, which Tim Zell saw as a magical craft or occult society, the CAW is intended to function as a public religion.

Gavin & Yvonne Frost found Church & School of Wicca in St Louis

Church of the Eternal Source is founded in Burbank, CA, by Donald Harrison, Harold Moss & Elaine Amiro as an Egyptian-revivalist Pagan group. (Aug. 25); registered with state of CA Oct 7.

NROOGD conducts first Eleusinian ritual on the autumnal equinox.

Aidan Kelly publishes a Pagan-Craft Calendar using the names "Litha" and "Mabon" for the summer solstice and fall equinox. The names are picked up by *Green Egg* and become standard among Pagans.

First public Witch-In held by Witches International Craft Associates (WICA) in New York's Central Park NYC's Central Park. It is attended by over 1,000 people.

Tim Zell has profound vision of the biosphere of Earth as a single vast living organism (Nov. 7). He writes it up and delivers his first sermon to the CAW: "TheaGenesis: The Birth of the Goddess."

1971 Susan B. Anthony #1 Coven founded in Venice, CA by Zsusanna Budapest. Dianic Witchcraft for women only.

Founding of the Pagan Front in the UK, which later changes its name to the Pagan Federation.

Aidan Kelly and other members of NROOGD meet Victor and Cora Anderson and the Faerie Tradition and NROOGD begin to influence each other.

Susan Roberts publishes *Witches USA.*

Patricia Crowther's radio show, *A Spell of Witchcraft,* airs in Britain.

Phillip Emmons Isaac Bonewits publishes *Real Magick.*

William Butler Gray publishes *Magical Ritual Methods.*

The Crystal Well begins publishing.

The first American Aquarian Festival of Astrology and the Occult Sciences, later called Gnosticon, is organized by Carl Weschcke and attended by many of the best-known Wiccans and Pagans. It is held in Minneapolis, MN. This leads to the creation of the American Council of Witches.

Fred Adams begins publishing Feraferia newsletter, *Korythalia.*

Tim Zell publishes "TheaGenesis: The Birth of the Goddess" in *Green Egg,* which articulates a Gaia-like theory several years before James Lovelock popularizes the idea.

Janet and Stewart Farrar leave Alex Sanders' coven to found their own coven. They become two of the most influential Wiccan authors, starting with the publication of *What Witches Do* in 1971.

Morgan McFarland and Mark Roberts create the Dianic Witchcraft tradition in Texas, now called McFarland Dianic, as distinguished from Z. Budapest's feminist Dianic witchcraft. Unlike Z. Budapest's Dianic tradition, the McFarland tradition is gender-inclusive in practice and theology.

Pictures of a NROOGD Beltane ritual appear in a *Look* magazine article entitled "Witches Are Rising."

Asatru is officially recognized as a religion by the government of Iceland.

1972 (Aug-Sept) Tim Zell and Julie tour California, weaving together many disparate strands into a self-aware network of Pagans. They win "Best of Show" in costume contest at LA Sci-Fi Worldcon as "Cernunnos & Cerridwen." A talk given by Julie to a women's group at the Worldcon is the beginning of the women's Goddess movement.

The UK-based Pagan Federation is organized.

The Council of Themis (Goddess of harmony) is disbanded, ironically due to internal conflicts.

1973 The Council of Earth Religions is established as successor to Council of Themis. Like its predecessor, it does not survive.

Joseph Wilson creates the 1734 Tradition.

Seax-Wicca Tradition is founded by Raymond Buckland.

Alison Harlow purchases Coeden Brith, a 220-acre Pagan sanctuary in California.

1974 Adoption of *The 13 Principles of Wiccan Belief* by the American Council of Witches at Gnostic Aquarian Festival in St. Paul, MN. At that event, Tim Zell and Morning Glory are married in the first public Pagan handfasting, conducted by Carolyn Clark and Isaac Bonewits, with Margot Adler singing (April 14).

The First Ecumenical Pagan Council is founded. Like its two predecessors, this council does not survive.

Raymond Buckland publishes *The Tree: The Complete Book of Saxon Witchcraft*, in which he reverses his earlier (1970) position on self-initiation. The same year, *Green Egg* publishes an article titled "How to Form Your Own Coven." This marks the beginning of the end of the hegemony of traditional Wicca in America.

Selena Fox founds Circle Wicca in Madison, Wisconsin, which becomes incorporated in 1978. It also begins the Pagan sanctuary movement.

WomanSpirit is first published, including articles, poetry, and rituals, exploring the Divine Feminine. Published until 1984.

Marija Gimbutas publishes *The Gods and Goddesses of Old Europe* (republished in 1982 as *The Goddesses and Gods of Old Europe*), which popularizes the theory of matriarchal prehistory.

1975 Covenant of the Goddess is chartered by Wiccan elders of various traditions as an umbrella organization for all Witchcraft practitioners. CoG is incorporated on Samhain as a non-profit religious organization in California.

Isaac Bonewits founds Aquarian Anti-Defamation League (AADL).

Glainn Sidhe Order of Witches founded by Andras Corben-Arthen

Doreen Valiente publishes *An ABC of Witchcraft*. She states that initiation is not necessary to become a witch.

Z Budapest publishes *The Feminist Book of Light and Shadows*, later republished as *The Holy Book of Women's Mysteries*. American Wicca becomes tied with the feminist spirituality movement.

Starhawk founds her Compost coven.

Gwydion Pendderwen releases his first album, *Songs for the Old Religion*. Establishes Annwfn, a 55-acre Pagan sanctuary in CA.

Fellowship of Isis established in Ireland by Rev. Lawrence Durdin-Robertson, Pamela Durdin-Robertson and the Hon. Olivia Robertson. It is dedicated to promoting all Goddess traditions.

The Philosophical Brotherhood of Druids founded in Brittany by Coaver Kalondan after a schism with the Breton gorsedd.

A Universal Fraternity of Druids is established in France, independently of the earlier groups

1976 The Aquarian Tabernacle Church is founded in WA by Pete Pathfinder Davis.

The Midwest Pagan Council is formed.

The Pan Pagan Festival is held in IN, the first national outdoor Pagan festival. 80 people attend. Within four years, the attendance grows to 600. Pagan festivals have since proliferated and led to the formation of a decentralized community with shared songs, dances, rituals, and culture.

Merlin Stone publishes *When God was a Woman*. It was published earlier in the U.K. as *The Paradise Papers: The Suppression of Women's Rites*.

Earth Religion News is published by Herman Slater.

1977 The Minoan Brotherhood, a Pagan tradition for gay men, is founded by Ed Buczynski.

Unitarian Universalist Association (UUA) publishes "Cakes for the Queen of Heaven," a 10-session workshop in feminist spirituality.

Joseph Bearwalker Wilson founds the Temple of the Elder Gods (TOTEG) as an attempt to discover locale-specific ways to worship one's ancestors and gods. The group is dissolved in 1988, but reconstituted in 1996 as Toteg Tribe, a Neo-Shamanic tradition.

Tim and Morning Glory Zell move to Alison Harlow's 220-acre Coeden Brith, adjacent to Gwydion Pendderwen's Annwfn.

1978 Darkmoon Circle is founded by Diana Paxson and Marion Zimmer Bradley.

The US Army publishes "Religious Requirements and Practices of Certain Selected Groups: A Handbook for Chaplains," which now includes chapters on Wicca and Witchcraft, but not other forms of Paganism.

Doreen Valiente publishes *Witchcraft for Tomorrow*, a complete Book of Shadows of her own composition, including a ritual for self-initiation.

Carol Christ gives keynote address at the University of California at Santa Cruz Extension Conference. Later published as "Why Women Need the Goddess" in *WomanSpirit Rising* (1979), it is the single most influential article in the Goddess movement.

Blue Star Wiccan tradition founded in Norristown, Penn. By Frank ("The Wizard") Dufner and Tzipora Katz.

1979 Conceived by Tim Zell, the largest magickal ritual in modern times celebrates total Solar Eclipse (Feb. 26) at full-scale Stonehenge replica in WA, attended by over 4,000 people. Group weather-working clears the clouds, resulting in major media publicity.

First Starwood Festival, sponsored by ACE (Association for Consciousness Exploration).

Starhawk publishes *The Spiral Dance*; becomes Neo-Pagan classic.

Margot Adler publishes *Drawing Down the Moon*. Adler's book together with Starhawk's become catalysts for the American Neo-Pagan movement.

Circle Sanctuary is founded in Wisconsin by Selena Fox and Jim Alan. It is covered by TIME magazine in an article entitled: "Religion: Preaching Pan, Isis, and Om." The article quotes J. Gordon Melton's estimate of 40,000 practicing Pagans. Selena Fox and other Pagans are later featured in a PBS documentary, *People* magazine, and other media. Coverage is positive.

Circle publishes Paganism's first networking sourcebook, *The Circle Guide to Wicca and Pagan Resources..*

The British Druid Order is founded by Phillip Shallcrass.

The EarthSpirit Community holds the first Rites of Spring.

1979 Starhawk and Diane Baker found Reclaiming in San Francisco, a tradition which draws on Anderson's Feri Tradition, Z Budapest's Dianic witchcraft, and the feminist, peace, and environmental movements.

1980 The largest Pagan festival to that time is held in Indiana, the Pan-Pagan Festival, sponsored by the Midwest Pagan Council and the Covenant of the Goddess. Almost 800 people attend the four-day festival. Z Budapest leads an all-women's circle which creates controversy and confrontation. The governing council then splits, forming three different organizations and festivals, including the Pagan Spirit Gathering led by Circle.

Circle Network News begins publishing.

Harvest magazine (1980-92).

Michael Harner publishes *The Way of the Shaman: A Guide to Power and Healing*, the first practical text on shamanism, introducing shamanic practices into Neo-Paganism.

EarthSpirit is founded by Andras Corban Arthen to provide networking for Pagans and others following an Earth-centered spiritual path.

1981 Janet and Stewart Farrar publish the Alexandrian Book of Shadows as *The Witches' Bible: The Complete Witches' Handbook*.

Pagan Spirit Gathering (PSG) holds its first annual week-long festival over the summer solstice.

1982 The Georgia Supreme Court rules, in Roberts v. Ravenwood Church of Wicca, that Wicca is a religion and that the Ravenwood church is entitled to tax exempt status.

Archeologist Marija Gimbutas republishes her 1974 book *The Gods and Goddesses of Old Europe* with the new name *The Goddesses and Gods of Old Europe*. She later publishes *The Language of the Goddess* (1989) and *The Civilization of the Goddess* (1991). With these books, she becomes the archaeologist most closely linked with the Goddess Movement.

Oaled Drwized Kornog (Hearth of the Western Druids) founded in Brittany by Goff ar Steredennou.

Goddess Rising conference in Sacramento, CA. Features Erica Jong and many Pagan luminaries.

Gwydion Pendderwen releases his 2nd album, The Faerie Shaman. At Samhain, he is killed in a car wreck, and Annwfn becomes the property of the Church of All Worlds.

1983 The Re-formed Congregation of the Goddess–International is incorporated and became the first legally recognized religion serving the women's spiritual community.

Isaac Bonewits forms *Ar nDraiocht Fein* (ADF) ("Our Own Druidism"), which eventually becomes the largest Neo-Druidic organization in North America.

The Encyclopedia of Man, Myth and Magic, edited by Richard Cavendish. An amazing 24-volume encyclopedia covering every conceivable topic.

1984 Janet and Stewart Farrar publish *The Witches Way*, which is strongly influenced by Jungian psychology.

1985 Three pieces of federal legislation, including the Helms Amendment, are introduced in both houses of Congress which would have taken away tax exempt status for Wiccan churches. Lady Liberty League emerges as a result of the nationwide networking that successfully defeats this legislation.

Witchcraft is legally recognized in the US. Dettmer v. Landon: the District Court of Virginia rules that Witchcraft falls within a recognizable religious category and **is** therefore protected by the Constitution.

The Covenant of Unitarian Universalist Pagans (CUUPS) is organized, providing education and credentials for Pagan clergy. CUUPS receives its charter from the UUA in 1987.

John and Caitlin Matthews begin publishing on Ceremonial magic, Arthurian and Celtic myth, and Neo-Shamanism. This could be considered the beginning of a non-denominational Neo-Paganism.

The use of the terms "Paganism," "Wicca" and "Magick" in published works marks the blossoming of what has been called "Generation Hex," a subgroup of Generation X.

Roger and Crystal Tier change the name of their New York Coven of *Caerlleuad* (Castle of the Moon) to the Gaia Group, reflecting its transformation into a more universal tradition, changing the names of its deities from Welsh to the "Great Earth Mother" and "Great Sky Father." Gaia Group ceases to exist in 1998.

Lady Liberty League is founded by Selena Fox and others. Sponsored by Circle Sanctuary, LLL is a resource center which promotes the religious freedom of Neo-Pagans and others.

1986 The UK band, the Pretenders, releases "Hymn to Her" which becomes #8 in the UK. The song, written by Meg Keane, is a Wiccan ode to the Goddess.

Witches League of Public Awareness is created by Laurie Cabot in Salem, MA to help correct the misconceptions surrounding Witches and Witchcraft.

Order of Bards, Ovates and Druids (OBOD) (founded in 1961) revived by Philip Carr-Gomm.

1987 Charles Arnold, formerly a member of the Wiccan Church of Canada, wins a legal battle in a Canada which results in the ruling that Wicca meets the definition of a religion.

Anne Niven begins publishing *Sagewoman* magazine.

1988 Scott Cunningham publishes *Wicca: A Guide for the Solitary Practitioner*, which becomes one of Llewellyn's best-selling publications. He is credited with making solitary practice respectable.

Otter Zell, Morning Glory Zell and Diane Darling resurrect the *Green Egg,* after a 10-year hiatus. It becomes the foremost Pagan journal—again.

Adoption of *The Earth Religion Anti-Abuse Resolution,* written by Morning Glory Zell, with over 100 signatory groups.

École Druidique des Gaules founded by the Allobragmatos, Boduogmatos and Catuvolus.

Fireheart magazine (1988-93)

1989 Crista Landon and Phaedra Christine Heyman (later Bonewits) found Panthea as a Pagan temple in Chicago in 1986. The congregation lasts until around 2003.

The Lycian Tradition of Wicca is founded.

Mezlim magazine (1989-95)

1990 20th anniversary of Earth Day on April 22 results in significant par-
      ticipation by Pagan groups.

      The Beltane issue of *Green Egg* (#90) publishes Morning's article,
      "A Bouquet of Lovers," in which she coins the word "poly-
      amorous," followed by "polyamory" and other derivative terms.

      Panthea becomes the first Pagan congregation of the Unitarian Uni-
      versalist Association of Congregations (UUA).

      Captain Planet animated series airs and lasts until 1996. Gaia
      (voiced by Whoopie Goldberg) is a prominent figure in the series.

      Cornardiia Druvidiacta Aremorica (Druid Brotherhood of Armor-
      ica) founded in Brittany after a split with the Kredenn Gieltiek.

1991 The World Wide Web begins to be popularized. An increase in the
      use of the Internet leads to the creation of many Pagan websites,
      driving the growth of non-traditional, eclectic, solitary, and teen
      Paganism.

      Aidan Kelly publishes *Crafting the Art of Magic* which casts serious
      doubt on the legitimacy of Gerald Gardner's claims to have been
      initiated into a survival of an ancient witchcraft religion.

      The Pan Pacific Pagan Alliance is founded by Julia Phillips and oth-
      ers, which later became The Pagan Alliance Inc., with a newsletter
      The Pagan Times, and branches in every state of Australia.

1992 The Church of All Worlds becomes the first legally recgnized Pagan
      church in Australia.

      The Druid Clan of Dana established in Ireland. It is founded on the
      work of the Fellowship of Isis.

1993 The Covenant of the Goddess is represented at the Parliament of the
      World's Religions at Chicago. The then-First Officer, Phyllis Cu-
      rott receives permission of Roman Catholic Archbishop Bernar-
      dino to hold a circle ceremony at a nearby park, in national press
      coverage for Pagans. Greek Orthodox delegation departs the Par-
      liament proceedings in protest over the very presence of Pagans.

      The Druidic Federation of Gaul founded by Pierre de la Crau out of
      the Druidic Church of Gaul and the Green Druidic Order of Ronan
      ap Lugh.

      The Insular Order of Druids is founded at Stonehenge by Dylan ap
      Thuinn.

      Order of Druids of Ireland is founded by Michael Mile McGrath.

      The first Panathenaia is conceived by Otter & Morning Glory Zell,
      and held at the Nashville Parthenon to dedicate the newly-com-
      pleted 42-ft. statue of Athena.

1994 *The Minneapolis Star Tribune* reports that the Twin Cities Metro-
      politan area has been dubbed "Paganistan" by Steve Posch.

The journal of the Pagan Federation changes its name from *The Wiccan* to *Pagan Dawn*, reflecting a broader Pagan membership.

Following his participation as Hades in the CAW Eleusinian Mysteries, Otter Zell is given new name of "Oberon."

1995 Several land-based Pagan sanctuaries founded: Camp Gaia, Brushwood, Heartspring, Mother Rest Sacred Grove, 4 Quarters Farm.

The Unitarian Universalist Assembly votes to acknowledge "Earth-centered" spirituality in its by-laws as a major source of UUA beliefs. Two years earlier, in 1993, the UUA included Goddess and Earth-centered songs in its new hymnal.

Actress Cybill Shepherd comes out as Pagan at the 1995 Golden Globe Awards, stating "And I want to thank the Great Mother Goddess of the gift of righteous anger and for all her strength and inspiration. Blessed be!" She later explains that she is a "Christian Pagan Buddhist Goddess worshiper" and a feminist.

1996 Witchcraft becomes televised with *Sabrina: the Teenage Witch*. The movie *The Craft* is released the same year and is credited with bringing many adolescents into Pagan Witchcraft.

Toteg is reconstituted by Joseph Wilson.

Oberon & Morning Glory Zell and their extended family move to 94-acre V-M Ranch, all taking last name of "Ravenheart."

1997 Wren Walker and Fritz Jung found WitchVox to be a Pagan resource center on the World Wide Web. The site grows to be the largest Pagan Internet site.

Pomegranate, the first academic journal of Pagan studies, is created.

The first non-Wiccan president of Pagan Federation is elected.

The Australian Pagan Awareness Network is founded to correct misinformation, raise awareness and educate the general public about Paganism.

J.K. Rowling's *Harry Potter and the Philosopher's Stone* is published. In 1997 and 1998; the television series *Buffy the Vampire Slayer* and *Charmed* air. These books, movies, and TV series portray characters who are openly witches, but not stereotypically evil. This also marks the beginning of an increasing commercialization of witchcraft.

1998 *Practical Magic* appears in theaters.

The first Pagan Pride Day is held in Indianapolis, IN.

1999 Ronald Hutton publishes *The Triumph of the Moon: A History of Modern Pagan Witchcraft*. His work arguably ends the controversy regarding the origin of Neo-Pagan witchcraft.

Last total Solar eclipse of the 2nd Millennium is celebrated at ancient stone circle of Boscan-ewen in Cornwall (Aug. 11). Conducting the rites are Andy Norfolk, Cassandra Latham, Oberon Zell, and others.

2000 A Dallas City Council invites a Wiccan to offer the invocation.

Oberon Zell convenes Committee of Pagan leaders and initiates "Papal Apology Project" to ask Pope to include Pagans in his Apology for horrors of Inquisition, etc. Over 6,000 signatures are gathered. Pope does apologize for "crimes against indigenous peoples."

In March, major "Pagan Leaders Summit" held in Indiana.

3rd Parliament of the World's Religions in South Africa. Many Pagan representatives attend, ally with traditional African shamans.

The 21st Century

2001 Jerry Falwell puts the blame for the 9-11 attacks on "Pagans, abortionists, feminists, gays and lesbians, the ACLU and others."

2002 *The Complete Idiot's Guide To ... Paganism* is published.

Rev. Angie Buchanan, director of Gaia's Womb, is elected to the Board of Trustees for the Council for a Parliament of the World's Religions, one of the most respected interfaith organizations in the world. In 2006, Andra Corban-Arthen, director of the EarthSpirit Community is elected. Then in 2009, Phyllis Curott, Pagan author and attorney is elected.\

Australian Census figures show rapid growth of Wicca and Paganism. Wiccans in Australia grew from fewer than 2,000 in 1996 to nearly 9,000 in 2001. The number of Pagans more than doubled over the same interval to 10,632. Most major Christian denominations lost followers over the same period.

2003 Canada releases religious data from the 2001 census which shows that Wiccans and other Pagans experienced the greatest percentage growth of all religions in the country. They numbered 21,080 members in 2001, an increase of 281% between 1991 and 2001. The percentage of Canadians identifying with Christianity dropped from 90% in 1981 to 72% in 2001 — about one percentage point per year. This drop is almost exactly the same in the U.S.

The Druid Network is organized in the UK to promote Druidry as a religion.

Oberon Zell assembles Grey Council to write *Grimoire for the Apprentice Wizard.*

2004 *Grimoire* published—enormously successful. OZ creates online Grey School of Wizardry (GSW—incorporated on "Pi Day," 3/14). GSW opens virtual doors on Lughnasadh (Aug. 1).

The Wild Hunt blog is relaunched by Jason Pitzl-Waters and becomes the lead voice for analysis and insight into how modern Pagan faiths are represented in mainstream media.

"Episcopagan" controversy breaks out when Glyn Ruppe-Melnyk and her husband W. William Melnyk, two Episcopalian ministers, are outed as members of a Druidic group after Ruppe-Melnyk submits a rite to the Episcopal Church's Women's Ministries website called "A Women's Eucharist."

Alta Mira Press launches the Pagan Studies series with *Researching Paganisms*, to be followed by Chas Clifton's *Her Hidden Children* in 2006 and Barbara Davy's *An Introduction to Pagan Studies* in 2007.

2005 An Indiana trial verdict that prohibited divorced Wiccan parents from exposing their 9-year-old son to "non-mainstream religious beliefs and rituals" is overturned on appeal.

Green Egg goes digital, edited by Ariel Monserrat and Tom Donohue.

Magick TV is founded on 11/11. The first show is "Pagan Nightly News."

2007 Cherry Hill Pagan Seminary is granted tax-exempt status. The seminary had been conducting online classes since 2000. It now offers several graduate degrees, certificates, and general courses.

The US Veteran's Administration approves the pentacle as #37 on the list of approved religious symbols on headstones for fallen soldiers in military cemeteries.

2009 The Sacred Paths Center opens in Minnesota. At the time, it is the only full-time non-profit Pagan community center in the U.S.

Ehoah (an offshoot of RDNA) is founded by Rua Lupa.

Aug. 24, Witch School Radio begins broadcasting with host Ed Hubbard.

"Pagans Tonight Radio Network" begins on Sept. 14, becoming the Voice of the Pagan World.

2010 The New Jersey Board of Education is the first to accept Pagan holidays as excused absences.

Brendan Myers and Jason Pitzl-Waters create a *Pagan Community Statement on Sexual Abuse,* 22 years after adoption of *The Earth Religion Anti-Abuse Resolution,* written by Morning Glory Zell.

2011 Debates surrounding transgender inclusiveness in Pagan spaces mark the beginning of a shift in Pagan consciousness regarding gender issues.

2012 Dec. 21. Aligned with the center of the galaxy, sunrise on Winter Solstice marks dawn of the Age of Aquarius.

2013   Thor's Hammer is approved for use on military headstones and grave markers.

Wicca and Paganism leave the Occult/New Age/Mind-Body-Spirit section of bookstore and move to the Religion section following a change in how books are coded.

2015   Nov. 28. Oberon Zell opens Academy of Arcana in Santa Cruz, CA, as physical space for Grey School of Wizardry. It lasts for 2 years.

2018   Oberon Zell embarks on 2-year "Walkabout of the Wandering Wizard," traveling throughout the Western Hemisphere.

2019   In recognition of the 60-year cycle of cultural renaissances, Oberon Zell launches the "2020 Vision" project.

Dec. 31. Witchvox, Pagandom's premier networking site, is retired after 22 years.

2020   Feb. Patheacon, the longest-running Pagan hotel conference, holds its final gathering after 25 years.

In the global COVID pandemic, live festivals are all canceled and Paganism goes virtual via Zoom. Paganism becomes recognized as a major world religion.

2021   Ed Hubbard and others launch "Pagan.World" as a successor to the retired Witchvox networking site. Oberon Zell is recruited as spokesman, with monthly Zoomcast: "The Ides of Oberon."

C.
thank goddess for pagans!

By Sivasiva Palani
Editor, *Hinduism Today*.
Feb. 1991

PAGAN. THE VERY WORD CONJURES UP uneasy feelings, and images of dancers in a moon-lit meadow or nearly-naked primitives. Yet every Hindu, all 900 million of us, is a Pagan. That's right. And if we knew the real meaning of the word, we would be proudly Pagan (though you might not have the machismo to wear the T-shirt that Orin Lyons, an Iroquois Indian chief and New York professor, designed proclaiming himself a "Born Again Pagan."

Webster defines Pagan as: "From the Latin *pagus,* a peasant, rustic. 1. A person who is not a Christian, Muslim or Jew; heathen: 2. A person who has no religion." Both Pagan and heathen apply to polytheistic peoples, though Pagan specifically refers to ancient peoples and traditions while heathen refers to any so-called primitive idolaters. Don't you just love Webster's implication that if you are not a Christian, Jew or Moslem, you have no religion?

Other etymologies – more interesting to Hindus, but less reliable – suggest as source the Greek root *pagos,* meaning "upright stone." Europe's early Pagans used the megaliths, large upright stones, in their rites. Today's neo-Pagans still use stones to honor the masculine Divine, just as we have worshipped the Sivalingam and Salagrama for millennia.

Researching this issue's page one story, I spoke to a few Pagans this week. They were all noticeably intelligent, informed and enthusiastic about their chosen faith, far more aware of what they believe than most Christians or Hindus are. Certainly they were more aware of Hinduism than our readers are likely to be about Paganism. Morning Glory Zell, a California-based Pagan leader, happily confessed that for seven years she has kept an altar to Lakshmi. Of several forms she has, a favorite is a painted image made from Ganges clay. She offers fresh flowers and water daily and performs puja, complete with sandalpaste, on holy days. She cherishes several dream visions of Ganesha and notes, "Most Pagans I know have at least one Hindu deity on their altar. Egyptian and Greek forms are also popular."

Morning Glory's husband, Otter, articulates their philosophy skillfully, "The Pagan theology is basically pantheism, the belief that all objects are given sacred significance. It has a universal outlook, one which embraces all indigenous folkways, one whose unifying vision keeps a place for all ethnic traditions. It is non-hierarchical, non-dogmatic and experiential, placing emphasis on unity through diversity."

Their numbers are small, resources modest and structure unstable. There are about 250,000 Pagans in the US. Most are what they term "solitaries," though more these days are joining groups, like the 200-member Church of All Worlds, founded in 1962 and federally tax-exempt since 1968.

Neo-Pagans possess a rich heritage of song, art, dance, mystery plays and poetry, mostly in English. Part of their liturgy comes from India. They commonly chant "Om" and sing hymns like Jai Ganesha or Kali Ma. Like Hindus, they follow a sacred calendar and place importance on the movement of the seasons and the cycles of sun and moon. Like Hindus, they decry the notion of a one true path, preferring to see God everywhere and in everyone. Like Hindus, Pagans hold personal enlightenment above faith or belief.

Aggressively suppressed by the Christians of Europe, Pagans were nearly exterminated. Even today they are under fire from fundamentalist Christians. They speak of losing their jobs, losing custody of their children in divorce proceedings, being falsely branded as satanic when they are in fact gentle, loving worshippers of nature.

Just as Hindus deplore the Nazi desecration of the auspicious swastika. Pagans lament the disparagement of the pentagram, a centuries-old symbol of their tradition. This five-sided insignia is a mark of man, arms outstretched, and a symbol of the heavenly star – Goddess Tara. Forces allied against the Pagans are linking the pentagram with demon worship and cultism. It is a false attack, but effective.

In reality, Pagans are nature worshippers, children of the Earth and devotees of the Goddess, the feminine divine. Religion to them centers on the natural world and cosmic entities, rather than a transcendent God. Pagans feel that Tibetan Buddhism is much attuned to them and count many Buddhists among their members. Otter Zell says, "We regard Hinduism as a sister religion from India. We both believe that the whole universe is a living, conscious entity." They find a similar kinship with Shinto. Attacked by Semitic faiths which ferociously repudiate polytheism, they want to forge alliances. We want them to know that Hinduism is a natural refuge and ally. Equally important is that they know this is possible without subtle reins on their independence or offense to their ways and wisdom.

Morning Glory has researched the occurrence of universal symbols – such as the unicorn, swastika, yin-yang and our own symbol for Himalayan Academy, the triskelion (the three-part logo at the bottom of this page). She has found these symbols in many places, distant in time and space, and concludes that the world's cultures share a single source, sort of a primeval path or perennial wisdom. "We have found the swastika in the arts of the pre-Indo-European Dravidians of India, the Tibetans, the Hopi Indians of the Americas, the European Pagans and others. It seems to be a sun symbol, and defines the four directions of the earth. It also represents the four elements, earth, air, fire and water."

Outside of the rural peoples of Europe, who are the great Pagans of history? They count Pythagoras and Archimedes, King Arthur and Chief Seattle. More broadly. Pagans would have to include the Druids (whom one man calls "the Brahmins of Europe") and American Indians. The Egyptians and Mayans. The Sumerians and Babylonians. The Romans and Greeks. The Polynesian tribes. The African peoples. The Japanese Shintos certainly qualify, as do the Chinese Taoists. The Tibetans, Indonesians, Nepalese and East Indians. The list is long. Being bold, we may count as Pagan the entire human race prior to the Christian era and all those following the Christian era but not following Christianity. Most of the human family, in other words.

Neo-Pagans look upon themselves as the first pluralists, the original Gaia hypothesizers, the deepest environmentalists. They revere and understand the Earth. They believe all things are alive, and all of life is related. Vision quests and direct encounter with the Divine are central to their path, thus they spend time in the wilderness, together or alone. Their ways (which can be eccentric, even weird) capture all that is human – the wisdom, humor, mysticism, vulnerability, strangeness, joy and spiritual drives that unify us.

There are resonances and common ground, but not everything called Pagan today is Hindu. Isaac Bonewits, priest of the Reformed Druids of America, says, "Hinduism is really paleo-Pagan. Like Taoism, it is the old, original Paganism, uncontaminated, existing before monotheism was created. The neo-Paganism of the last 30 or 40 years is a sincere reconstruction, but filled with romantic fantasy, making it the distant cousin of Hinduism, 16 times removed."

Still, Morning Glory's bottom line is apt, "We are all reaching into the self, seeking to touch the Gods within us."

δ.
"we are the other people"

By Oberon Zell

DING-DONG!" GOES THE DOORBELL. IS IT Avon calling? Or perhaps Ed McMahon with my three million dollars? No, it's the Yahweh's Witlesses again, just wanting to have a nice little chat about the Bible...

Boy, did they ever come to the wrong house! So we invite them in: "Enter freely and of your own will..." Diane and I amuse ourselves watching the expressions on the two young men as they check out the living room: ceremonial masks and medicine skulls of dragons and unicorns on the walls; crystals, wands, staffs, swords; lots of Goddess figures and several altars; posters and paintings of wizards and dinosaurs and witchy women; very many books, most of them dealing with obviously weird subjects... To say nothing of the great horned owl perched on the back of my comfy chair and the Unicorn grazing in the front yard. You know; early Addams Family decor.

And then Morning Glory comes wandering out naked, looking for her wake-up cup of tea. Morning Glory naked is a truly impressive sight, and the Witlesses look as if she'd set titties on stun as they stand immobilized, hands clasped over their genitals. With the stage set and all the actors in place, the show is ready to begin.

Their mission, of course, it to save our heathen souls by turning us on to "The Word of the Lord"—their Bible. I guess they figure some of us just haven't heard about it yet, and we're all eagerly awaiting their joyous tidings of personal salvation through giving our rational faculties to Jesus. Every time they come around, I look forward to trying out a new riposte. Sure, it may be cruel and sadistic of me, but hey, I didn't call them up and ask them to come over; they entered at their own risk!

After letting them run off their basic rap while lovely naked Morning Glory serves us all hot herb tea, I innocently remark: "But none of that applies to us. We have no need for salvation because we don't have original sin. We are the Other People."

"Hunh? What?" they reply eloquently. It's clear they've never heard this one before.

"Right," I say. "It's all in your Bible." And I proceed to tell them the story, using their own book for reference:

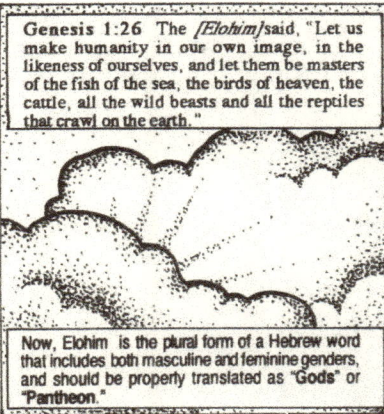

Genesis 1:26 The *[Elohim]* said, "Let us make humanity in our own image, in the likeness of ourselves, and let them be masters of the fish of the sea, the birds of heaven, the cattle, all the wild beasts and all the reptiles that crawl on the earth."

Now, Elohim is the plural form of a Hebrew word that includes both masculine and feminine genders, and should be properly translated as "**Gods**" or "**Pantheon**."

Gen. 1:27 The Gods created humanity in the image of Themselves. In the image of the Gods, they created them. Male and female They created them.

1:28 The Gods blessed them, saying to them, "Be fruitful, multiply, fill the earth and conquer it. Be masters of the fish of the sea, the birds of heaven and all living animals on the earth."

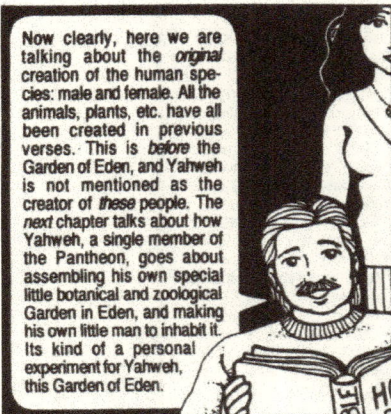

Now clearly, here we are talking about the *original* creation of the human species: male and female. All the animals, plants, etc. have all been created in previous verses. This is *before* the Garden of Eden, and Yahweh is not mentioned as the creator of *these* people. The *next* chapter talks about how Yahweh, a single member of the Pantheon, goes about assembling his own special little botanical and zoological Garden in Eden, and making his own little man to inhabit it. Its kind of a personal experiment for Yahweh, this Garden of Eden.

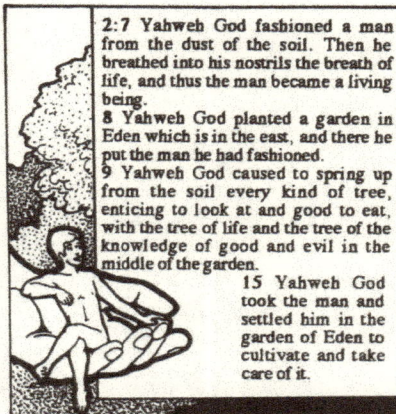

2:7 Yahweh God fashioned a man from the dust of the soil. Then he breathed into his nostrils the breath of life, and thus the man became a living being.

8 Yahweh God planted a garden in Eden which is in the east, and there he put the man he had fashioned.

9 Yahweh God caused to spring up from the soil every kind of tree, enticing to look at and good to eat, with the tree of life and the tree of the knowledge of good and evil in the middle of the garden.

15 Yahweh God took the man and settled *him* in the garden of Eden to cultivate and take care of it.

7

Now this next is crucial: note Yahweh's precise words:

16 Then Yahweh God gave the man this admonition: "You may eat indeed of all the trees in the garden.

17 Nevertheless of the tree of The Knowledge of Good and Evil you are *not* to eat, for on the day you eat of it, *you shall most surely die.*"

Fateful words, those. We will refer back to this admonition a little bit later on in the story.

DO NOT EAT!

Then Yahweh decides to make a woman to go with the man. Now, don't forget that the Pantheon had earlier created a whole *population* of people, "male and female," who are presumably doing just fine somewhere "outside the gates of Eden." But this little experiment will unfold to its own destiny.

21 So Yahweh God made the man fall into a deep sleep. And while he slept, he took one of his ribs and enclosed it in flesh.
22 Yahweh God built the rib he had taken from the man into a woman, and brought her to the man.
   Yeah. Right. The little man gives birth to a woman. *Sure* he does. But anyway, that's the way this story is told in the Bible.

25 Now both of them were naked, the man and his wife, but they felt no shame in front of each other.

Well, of course not! Why should they? But take careful note of those words, as they also will soon prove to be significant...

Now this next part is where it starts to get interesting.   Enter the Serpent:

Gen. 3:1 The serpent was the most subtle of all the wild beasts that Yahweh God had made. It asked the woman, "Did God really say you were not to eat from any of the trees in the garden?"
2 The woman answered the serpent, "We may eat of the fruit of the trees in the garden.
3 "But of the fruit of the trees in the middle of the garden God said 'You must not eat nor touch it, under pain of death.'"

9

4 Then the serpent said to the woman, "Ye shall not surely die.
5 "God doth know that on the day ye eat of it, your eyes shall be opened, and ye shall be as gods, knowing good and evil."

What a remarkable statement! "Your eyes shall be opened, and ye shall be as gods, knowing good and evil." The serpent directly contradicts Yahweh.
   Obviously, they both can't be right, so one of them must be lying. Which one, do you suppose?
   And, if the serpent speaks true, wouldn't you wish to eat of this magic fruit? Wouldn't it be a good thing, to become "like gods, knowing good and evil?"
   Or is it preferable to remain in ignorance? That idea deserves a little thought!

HOLY

6 The woman saw that the tree was good to eat and pleasing to the eye, and that it was also desirable for the knowledge that it could give. So she took some of the fruit and did eat, giving also to her husband who was with her, and he did eat.

7 And the eyes of them both were opened, and they knew that they were naked; and they sewed fig leaves together and made themselves aprons.

The author makes an interesting assumption here: that if you realize that you are naked, you will want to cover yourself. Further implications will unfold shortly...

Then the man and his wife hid amongst the trees.

9 But Yahweh God called to the man. "Where are you?" he asked.

10 "I heard thy voice in the garden," he replied. "I was afraid because I was naked, so I hid myself."

11 "Who told thee thou wast naked?" he asked. "Hast thou eaten the fruit of the forbidden tree?"

And so the sign of the fall becomes shame. Take note of this. The decendants of Adam and Eve will be distinguished throughout history from virtually all other peoples by their obsessive body taboos, and will feel shamed at being naked. It follows that those who feel no shame in being naked are, by definition, not carriers of this hereditary disease of Original Sin.

11

And now we come to the crux of The Fall. Yahweh had said back there in Gen.2-17 regarding the fruit of the Tree of Knowledge, that "On the day you eat of it you shall surely die." The serpent, on the other hand, had contradicted Yahweh in chapter 3:4-5: "Ye shall not surely die" and "God doth know that on the day ye eat of it, your eyes shall be opened, and ye shall be as gods, knowing good and evil." So what actually happened? Who lied, and who told the truth about this magical fruit? The answer is given in the next verse:

22 Then Yahweh God said, "See, the man has becomeas one of *us* to know good and evil. He *must* not be allowed to stretch forth his hand next and eat of the Tree of Life also, and live forever."

Isn't that curious? Why not, I wonder?

Get that? Yahweh himself *admits* that he *lied!* In fact, and *in Yahweh's own words,* the serpent spoke the absolute truth! And moreover, Yahweh tells the rest of the gods that he intends to evict Adam (and presumably, Eve as well) to *keep them* from gaining *immortality* to go with their newly-acquired divine knowledge. To prevent them, in other words, *from truly becoming gods!* So who, in this story, comes off as the benefactor of humanity, and who comes off as a tyrant? *THE SERPENT NEVER LIED!*

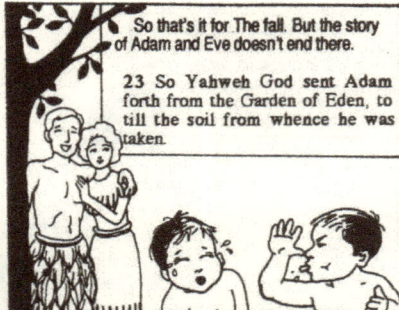

So that's it for The fall. But the story of Adam and Eve doesn't end there.

23 So Yahweh God sent Adam forth from the Garden of Eden, to till the soil from whence he was taken.

Gen. 4:1 And Adam knew his wife, and she conceived and bore Cain...

3 And again she bore his brother, Abel. Now Abel became a shepherd and kept flocks, and Cain was a tiller of the ground.

13

3 And in time it came to pass, Cain brought of the fruits of the soil, and made an offering to Yahweh.
4 While Abel brought of the firstborn of his flock, and of their fat.

Yahweh looked with favor on Abel and his offering, but did not look with favor on Cain, and he became angry and downcast.

Well, wouldn't *you* be? Both brothers had brought forth their first fruits as offerings, but Yahweh rejected the vegetables and *only* accepted the *blood sacrifice*. This was to set a gruesome precedent

8 Cain said to his brother Abel, "Let us go out;" and while they were in the fields, Cain set upon his brother Abel and slew him.

Accursed and marked a murderer, 16 Cain went from the presence of Yahweh, and dwelt in the land of Nod, east of Eden. Implicit in the phrase "went from the presence of Yahweh" is that Yahweh was only a local deity and not omnipresent. Now Eden, according to Gen.2:14-15, was situated at the mouth of the Euphrates and Tigris rivers where the Arabian Gulf is now. "East of Eden," therefore, would be somewhere along the shores of the Caspian Sea, in the Indo-European heartland. Cain settled there, among the people of Nod, and married one of the local women. Here is the first time "the other people" are mentioned, the Pagans, who are not of Adam and Eve's line.

So let's look at this story from another viewpoint. There we were, around six thousand years ago, living in our little farming community on the Caspian Sea, in the land of Nod, when this boy with a terrible scar comes stumbling out of the sunset. He tells us this bizarre story about how his mother and father had been created by a god named Yahweh, put in charge of a beautiful garden somewhere out west, and how they got banished for eating some of the god's magic fruit. He told us of murdering his brother, as this god would only accept blood sacrifice, and receiving that awful scar from him as a mark so that all would know him as a murderer.

He seems to believe that he is tainted by the "sin" of his parents' disobedience; that somehow it is in his blood, and will continue to contaminate his children and his children's children. One of our healing women takes pity, and marries him...

17 And Cain knew his wife, and she conceived and bore Enoch; and he built a city, and called it after his son, Enoch.

Well, with their only surviving son so far turning out not very well, Adam and Eve decided to try again:

25 Adam knew his wife again, and she bore a son and called him Seth...

26 A son was also born to Seth, and he called him Enos; then began men to call upon the name of the Yahweh God.

195

"OtheR PeOpLe" pOstsCRIpt:

Well, the story goes on, and maybe next time the Witlesses come to visit I'll tell more of it. But suffice it to say that those of us who are not of Semitic descent (i.e., not of the lineage of Adam and Eve) cannot share in the Original Sin that comes with that lineage. Being that the Bible is the story of that lineage, of Adam and Eve's descendants and their special relationship with their particular god, Yahweh, it follows that this is not the story of the rest of us. We may have been Cain's wife's people, or Seth's wife's people, or some other people over the hill and far away, but whichever people the rest of us are, as far as the Bible is concerned, we are the Other People, and so we are continually referred to throughout.

Later books of the Bible are filled with admonitions to the followers of Jahweh to *"learn not the ways of the pagans..."* (Jer. 10:2) with detailed descriptions of exactly what it is we do, such as erect standing stones and sacred poles; worship in sacred groves; practice divination and magick; note the movements of the sun, moon and stars—and burn incense and offer cakes to the "Queen of Heaven." (Jer. 7:18)

"You must not behave as they do in Egypt where once you lived; you must not behave as they do in Canaan where I am taking you. You must not follow their laws." (Lev 18:3) For Yahweh, as he so clearly emphasizes, is *not* the god of the Pagans. We have our own lineage and our own heritage, and our tale is not told in the Bible.

We were not "made" like clay figurines by a male deity out of "dust from the soil." We were born of our Mother the Earth, and have evolved over aeons in Her nurturing embrace. All of us, in our many and diverse tribes, have creation myths and legends of our origins and history; some of these tales may even be actually true. Like the descendants of Adam and Eve, many of us also have stories of great floods, earthquakes, volcanic eruptions and other cataclysms that wiped out whole communities of our people, wherein "I alone survived to tell the tale."

Nearly all of our ancestral tribes (and especially those of us who today are reclaiming our own Pagan heritage) lack that peculiar obsessive body modesty that seems to be a hallmark of the original sin alluded to in the story of the Fall. We can be naked and unashamed! Why, our Goddess even tells us, "as a sign that you are truly free, you shall be naked in your rites." Not being born into sin, we have no need of salvation, and no need of a Messiah to redeem our sinful souls. Neither heaven nor hell is our destination in the afterlife; we have our own various arrangements with our own various deities. The Bible is not our story; we have our own stories to tell, and they are many and diverse. Collect the whole set!

Green Egg, Vol. XXII, No. 85 (Beltane 1989) pp. 12-14

E.
Index of pagan paths

Some notable Neo-Pagan organizations
(NEW AGE, ECLECTIC, SYNCRETIC, ECUMENICAL...)

Eclectic Paganism
Goddess movement
Neoshamanism

- **Adocentyn Research Library**, San Francisco, CA (2011). https://adocentynlibrary.org/
- **American Council of Witches, Pagans, and friends** (1973). www.facebook.com/groups/northamericancouncilofwitchespagans-andfriends
- **Ardantane.** NM (1996). www.ardantane.org
- **Assembly of the Sacred Wheel,** Georgetown, DE (1984; incorp. 1985). www.sacredwheel.org
- **Bay Area Pagan Alliance (BAPA).** https://business.facebook.com/thePaganalliance/
- **Buckland Museum of Magick,** Cleveland, OH (1966; 2015). https://bucklandmuseum.org/
- **Cherry Hill Seminary,** SC (2001). www.cherryhillseminary.org/
- **Church of All Worlds (CAW)** (1962; incorp. 1968), publishes *Green Egg* (1968-present). www.CAW.org
  - **CAW Australia** (1992). http://www.caw.org.au/
- **Circle Sanctuary,** Mt Horeb, WI (1974); newsletter, *Circle Network News*, ceased publication in 2017. www.circlesanctuary.org
- **Council of Magickal Arts (CMA)**, TX (1980). www.magickal-arts.org
- **Covenant of Unitarian Universalist Pagans (CUUPS)** (1985). www.CUUPS.org
- **Discordians** (1963). https://en.wikipedia.org/wiki/Discordianism
- **EarthSpirit** (1977). www.earthspirit.com/
- **Fellowship of Isis** (Ireland) (1976). http://www.fellowshipofisis.com/
- **Feri Tradition** (1960). https://en.wikipedia.org/wiki/Feri_Tradition
- **Free Spirit Alliance (FSA)** (1986). http://freespiritalliance.org/
- **GaiaStar Temple & Blue Lotus Mystery School,** Cascadia, WA (2021) www.gaiastartemple.org
- **Gaia's Temple**, Shoreline, WA (2000). www.gaiastemple.org/
- **Harmony Tribe** (1997), Finlayson, MN. www.harmonytribe.org
- **Heartland Spiritual Alliance**, Lawrence, KS (1985). https://kchsa.com/

- **Midwest Pagan Council** (1976). www.midwestpagancouncil. org/
- **New Alexandrian Library,** Georgetown, DE. www.newalexandrian-library.com/
- **Pagan Federation**, UK (1971). www.PaganFed.org
- **The Pagan Way** (1969). www.facebook.com/groups/pagan.way
- **Pagan.World** (2021). https://paganworld.com
- **Radical Faeries** (1998) www.radfae.org
- **Reclaiming** (1979). https://reclaimingcollective.wordpress.com/
- **SisterSpirit**, Portland, OR (1985). http://www.sisterspiritwomensharing spirituality.org/
- **Universal Pantheist Society** (1975), http://network.pantheist.net/
- **Vegas Vortex**, Las Vegas, NV www.VegasVortex.com
- **Venusian Church**, Redmond, WA (1978). https://venusian.church/
- **The Wisdom School & Temple of Sophia**, Montague, MA. www.schoolofsophia.com/
- **Witch School**, Chicago, IL (2001). https://witchschool.com/
- **Wite Rayvn Metaphysical Church**, MO (2009). witerayvn.org/

Wicca/Witchcraft

Wiccan Churches (incorporated)
- **Aquarian Tabernacle Church (ATC)**, Index, WA (1979). www.atcwicca.org
- **Assembly of the Sacred Wheel**, Georgetown, DE (1984). http://www.sacredwheel.org/
- **Church and School of Wicca** (1968). https://wicca.org/
- **Circle Sanctuary**, WI (1974). www.CircleSanctuary.org
- **Corellian Nativist Church**, Albany, NY (1479). http://correl-lian.weebly.com/
- **Covenant of the Goddess (COG)** (1975). https://cog.org/
- **New Reformed Orthodox Order of the Golden Dawn (NROOGD)** (1968)
- **People of the Woods Church of the Old Religion** (2017), Cheney, WA. http://www.oldways.org/
- **Rowan Tree Church** (1979). www.therowantreechurch.org
- **Southern Delta Church of Wicca**, Lake City, AR (1994) www.facebook.com/SDCW.ATC/
- **Temple of the Nine Wells,** Salem, MA. https://business.facebook.com/thetempleofninewellsatc
- **Temple of Witchcraft**, Salem, NH (2009). www.templeofwitchcraft.org

British Traditional Wicca (BTW)

o Algard Wicca (1972)
o Alexandrian Wicca (1967)
o Blue Star Wicca (1975)
o Central Valley Wicca (1969)
o Chthonioi Alexandrian Wicca (1974)
o Gardnerian Wicca (1954)

Other Wiccan Traditions

o 1734 Tradition
o Appalachian
o Cabot Wicca
o Celtic Wicca
o Children of Artemis
o Christian Wicca
o Church of Wicca
o Cochrane's Craft
o Conjure Craft
o Coven of Atho
o Coven of the Far-Flung Net (1998)
o Deboran Craft of the Wise
o Dianic Wicca
o Druidic Craft of the Wise
o Eclectic Wicca
o Faery Wicca
o Feri Tradition
o Georgian Wicca
o Hedge Witchcraft
o Inclusive Wicca
o McFarland Dianic Wicca
o Mosian Wicca
o Odyssean Wicca
o Reclaiming
o Saxon Wicca
o Seax-Wica
o Universal Eclectic Wicca

Ethnic/Reconstructionist/Revivalist Paganism

Polytheistic reconstructionism
European Congress of Ethnic Religions

African & Afro-Caribbean
o Candomblé
o Ifa (Nigeria)
o Santeria
o Vodun

Baltic
o Dievturība (Latvian)
  - Community of Latvian Dievturi (1926–early 1930s)
  - Congregation of Latvian Dievturi (1927–1940)
  - Latvian Church Dievturi (1971)
  - Congregation of Latvian Dievturi (1990)
o Romuva (Lithuanian Pagan Society) (1992), based on pre-1387 Lithuanian Paganism. http://romuva.lt/

Canarian
o Church of the Guanche People

Caucasian
Caucasian neoPaganism
o Abkhaz neoPaganism
  - Council of Priests of Abkhazia (2012)
o Adyghe Habze
o Vainakh religion

Celtic/Druidry
Celtic Reconstructionist Paganism (1980s)
Neo-Druidism or Neodruidry
o Ancient Order of Druids in America (1874)
o Archaeological Order of Druids Dynion Mwyn (1950s/60s)
o Ár nDraíocht Féin (ADF), A Druid Fellowship (1983). www.ADF.org
  ▪ Stone Creed Grove, ADF, Cleveland, OH. www.stonecreed.org
o The Druid Order (1909). http://thedruidorder.org/
o Keltic Orthodox Church of the Order of the Royal Oak, TN (1988). www.AvalonIsle.org
o Order of Bards, Ovates & Druids (OBOD), UK (1964). druidry.org
o Reformed Druids of North America (RDNA) (1963). http://rdna.info/
o Tribe of the Oak (*Tuatha na Dara*), MA (2014). www.tribeoftheoak.com
o Weald Workers of Lamar County, Paris, TX (2020). www.facebook.com/WealdWorkers.

Germanic/Norse/Heathenry

Heathenism (also Heathenry, or Greater Heathenry), is a blanket term for the whole Germanic NeoPagan movement. Various currents and denominations have arisen over the years within it. A significant and problematic faction (mainly Odinists—whom I have omitted from this Index) embrace white supremacy, necessitating a disavowal by other Heathens (mainly Asatruar). The non-racist organizations that signed Declaration 127 to promote "inclusive Heathenry" are:

- Forn Sidr of America - Social Action
- Heathens Against Hate - Social Action
- Hvergelmir International - Networking
- The Troth - Educational
- The Asatru Community - Social Action

o Asatru
  - Ásatrú Alliance (AA), AZ (1988)
  - Asatru Community. www.theasatrucommunity.org/
  - International Asatru-Odinic Alliance (1997–2002)
  - Mannaheim Kindred (VA). www.independent-kindred.org/
  - The Troth (1987), publishes *Idunna*. www.TheTroth.org
- Scandinavia
  o Íslenska Ásatrúarfélagið (1972)
  o Forn Sed Norge (1998)
  o Samfälligheten för Nordisk Sed (1999)
  o Swedish Asatru Assembly (1994)
  o Åsatrufelsskapet Bifrost (1996)
- German-speaking Europe
  o Eldaring (2000)
- Russian-speaking world/Russia
  o Dark Ashtree community
  o Скидбладнир
- Germanic mysticism (*Armanism* or *Irminism/Irminenschaft*/Ariosophy and Nordic racial Paganism
  o Heidnische Gemeinschaft (1985)
  o Artgemeinschaft (1951)
  o Deutsche Heidnische Front (1998)
  o New Armanen-Orden

Hawaiian
o Huna

Hellenic (Greek) Paganism
Hellenism (revival of Ancient Greek religion)
o   Elaion (2005). http://elaion.org/
o   Feraferia (1967), established in CA by Frederick M. Adams as a continuation of his Fellowship of Hesperides (1957). http://Feraferia.org
o   Hellenion (2001). www.hellenion.org/
o   Labrys (2008) (Greek with some text in English) www.labrys.gr/gr/
o   Orphism, https://www.hellenicgods.org/
o   Thiasos Olympikos (1989) home.pon/rhinoceroslodge/thiasos.htm
o   Societas Hellenica Antiquariorum (English)
o   Sodalitas Graecia (English and Greek)
o   Supreme Council of Ethnikoi Hellenes (YSEE) (1997) (English). www.ysee.gr/index-eng.php
    ▪ Australian Ethnikoi Hellenes (branch of YSEE)
    ▪ Hellenes Ethnikoi in Canada (branch of YSEE)
    ▪ Supreme Council of National Greeks America (YSEE)
o   Thyrsos - Hellenes Ethnikoi (Greek and English). www.thyrsos.gr/
o   United Hellenismos Association. https://m.facebook.com/UnitedHellenismosAssociation/

Hindu (India)
o   The Indian School of Natural Spiritual Science, India. www.theindianschoolofnaturalspiritualsciences.com

Kemetic (Egyptian)
Kemetism
o   Ausar Auset Society (1973). https://ausarausetatl.com/aasintl
o   Church of the Eternal Source (1970) https://sites.google.com/site/churcheternalsource/
o   Kemetic Orthodoxy (1988). www.Kemet.org
o   Fellowship of Isis, Clonegal Castle, Ireland (1976). www.fellowshipofisis.com/

Native American
o   Buffalo Trace Society, Spokane, WA. https://www.meetup.com/Buffalo-Trace-Society/
o   Mexicayotl (1950s). https://slife.org/mexicayotl/
o   Native American Church (late 19th century). https://web.archive.org/web/20050308162749/http://www.utah-nac.org/nacindex.html
o   Pachamama Alliance, San Francisco, CA. https://www.pachamama.org/

- o Pacific Northwest Wolf Clan (2013), Spokane, WA. https://www.facebook.com/groups/477228735698972/

Roman/Italic
Italo-Roman neoPaganism or *Religio Romana*
- o Nova Roma (1998). http://www.novaroma.org/
- o Roman Traditional Movement
- o Stregheria (Italian)

Semitic
- o Semitic neoPaganism

Shinto (Japan)

Slavic
- o Rodnovery (Native Faith) (1920–30s)
  - • Native Ukrainian National Faith, RUNVira (1964)
  - • Peterburgian Vedism
- o Union of the Veneds (1986)
  - • Ynglism (1991)
  - • Native Polish Church (1995)
  - • Rodzima Wiara (1996)
  - • Union of Slavic Native Belief Communities (1997)
  - • Rodnover Confederation (2015)
  - • Commonwealth of Pagan Communities of Siberia–Siberian Veche (2015)
- o Zadruga (1937)
- o Ivanovism (1930s)
- o Tezaurus Spiritual Union (Authentism) (1984)
- o Russian national movement–Course of Truth and Unity (Conception of Social Security–Dead Water) (1985)
- o Bazhovism (1992)
- o Ringing Cedars' Anastasianism (1997)

Turko-Mongolic
- o Aar Aiyy Faith (Yakut: Аар Айыы итэҕэлэ) (1996)
- o Aiyy Faith (Yakut: Айыы итэҕэлэ), former Kut-Siur (1990)
- o Aiyy Tangara Faith (Yakut: Айыы Таҥара итэҕэлэ) (2019)
- o Burkhanism/Ak Jang (Altay: Ак јаҥ) (1904)
- o International Fund of Tengri Research (Russian: Международный Фонд Исследования Тенгри) (2011)

204   Goodbye Jesus, I've gone home to Mother

- o Mongolian shamanism/Tengerism (Mongolian: Бөө мөргөл/Тэнгэризм)
  - Heaven's Dagger
  - Mongolian Shamans' Association (Golomt Tuv)
    - o Circle of Tengerism (Mongolian shamanic association of America)
    - o Golomt Center for Shamanist Studies
  - Samgaldai Center (Mongolian: Хаант Тэнгэрийн Самгалдай)
- o Tengir Ordo (Kyrgyz: Теңир Ордо) (2005)
- o Vattisen Yaly (Chuvash: Ваттисен йӑли)
  - Chuvash National Congress (Chuvash: Чӑваш наци конгресĕ) (1989–1992)
  - Chuvash Traditional Faith Organization "Tura" (Russian: Организация традиционной веры чувашей "Тура") (1995)

Uralic
Uralic neoPaganism
- o Estonian neoPaganism (*Taaraism* and *Maausk*)
  - Maavalla Koda (1995)
- o Finnish neoPaganism
- o Hungarian neoPaganism
- o Mari native religion
- o Mordvin native religion
- o Udmurt Vos

Other European
- o Armenian Native Faith (Hetanism)
- o Assianism (Ossetian Native Faith)
- o Zalmoxianism

MAJOR PAGAN FESTIVALS (USA) – *LISTED BY MONTH*

NOTE: Nearly all Pagan groups celebrate some version of the eight-spoked "Wheel of the Year," with festive ritual gatherings every six weeks at the Solstices, Equinoxes, and cross-quarters midway between. Multiply the numbers of all the groups listed here (and all those not listed) by 8, and you'll realize the impossibility of listing all of them. Here is a short list of the larger and more public Pagan festivals in the US. But keep in mind that if, say, a Beltane festival is listed for some group, that same group probably also hosts several more festivals throughout the year!

Jan. **Between the Worlds,** every several years since 1996. www.sacredwheel.org/

Jan. **Sacred Space Conference,** DC/Baltimore, since 2014. www.sacredspacefoundation.org/

Feb. **A Feast of Lights** (formerly **HearthFire**), MA, since 1989. http://www.earthspirit.com/events/a-feast-of-lights

Feb. **Hawkfest Drum and Dance Gatherings,** Bonita Springs, FL. https://www.facebook.com/groups/175031977219/

Feb. **Mysterium,** Las Vegas, NV. www.vegasvortex.com/vegas-vortex-events/mysterium-event/

Mar. **Mystical Minds Convention**, Comfort Inn, Newark, CA. https://mysticalmindsconvention.com/

Mar. **PaganiCon,** Minneapolis, MN, since 2011. https://paganicon.org/

Mar. **Spring Mysteries Festival,** WA, since 1986. www.springmysteries.com

Mar. **Phoenix Phyre,** Solomon Springs, Bell, FL, since 1992. www.phoenixfestivals.com/

Apr. **Fertile Ground Gathering**, Triangle, VA. www.fertilegroundgathering.com

Apr. **Trillium Spring Gathering** (ADF), Cross Junction, VA, since 2005. registration@trilliumgatheringadf.org

May. **Beltaine**, Our Haven, French Lick, IN. www.ourhaven.info

May **Beltania**, All World Acres, Tampa, FL. http://healingtoday.com/beltainia.htm

May **CAW Beltaine**, Annwfn, Redwood Valley, CA, since 1983. https://annwfn.org/

May **CMA Beltane**, Spirit Haven Ranch (CMA), Flatonia, TX, since 1980. www.magickal-arts.org/

May **Gathering of All Paths**. www.facebook.com/groups/193357044355976/

May **Heartland Pagan Festival,** Gaea Retreat Center, McLouth, KS, since 1986. https://kchsa.com/heartland-pagan-festival/

May **Horn & Honey**, Midian, Springville, IN. www.hornandhoney.com

May **Ishtarfest**, central NJ. https://handsofchangenj.wordpress.com/ishtarfest

May **Mayfire**, Las Vegas, NV. www.vegasvortex.com/vegas-vortex-events/mayfire-event/

May **May Moon Magick**, Cosby, TN. www.facebook.com/events/cerren-ered/may-moon-magick

May **Moondance**, Roxanna, Auburn, AL. http://www.faeriefaith.net/Moondance.shtml

May **PanGaia Festival,** Sacramento, CA since 2015. https://pangaiafestival.com/

May **Rites of Spring,** MA, since 1979. www.earthspirit.com/events

May **Walpurgisnacht**, Lewisburg TN. http://www.walpurgis-nachtevent.com/

May **Wellspring Gathering** (ADF), Tredara, Cleveland, OH, www.stonecreed.org/wellspring

May **Wyld Fire Beltane Hunt**, Gryphon's Nest Campground, Springfield LA. https://www.wyldfirehunt.com/

June **Appalachian Summer Solstice**, Wisteria, Pomeroy, OH. www.wisteria.org/events/summer-solstice/

June **Babalon Rising Pan-Thelemic Festival**, Camp Midian, Springville, IN. www.babalonrising.com

June **California Witchcamp**, *Mendocino Woodlands, NorCA.* www.californiawitchcamp.org/

June **Chrysalis Moon**, Rising Sun Campground, Knox, IN. www.chrysalismoon.com

June **Elf-Fest**, Lothlorien Nature Sanctuary, Bedford/Needmore, IN. https://elvinhome.org/elf-fest/

June **Free Spirit Gathering,** Camp Ramblewood, Darlington, MD. www.fsgonline.org/

June **Michigan Pagan Festival**, Wayne County Fairgrounds, Belleville, MI. www.michiganpaganfestival.com/

June **Pagan Spirit Gathering,** Waynesville, MO, since 1980. www.circlesanctuary.org/index.php/pagan-spirit-gathering/pagan-spirit-gathering

June **Pagan Unity Festival,** Montgomery Bell State Park, Burns, TN, since 1997. www.paganunityfestival.org/

June **St. Louis Pagan Picnic,** St Louis, MO, since 1992. www.paganpicnic.org/

June **Three Gates Gathering**, West Plains, MO http://threegatesgathering.com/

July **Pan Pagan Festival,** Knox, IN, since 1976. www.midwestpagancouncil.org/festival.html

July **Sirius Rising,** Sherman, NY, since 1994. www.brushwood.com/sirius-rising

July **SpiritFire,** New Lebanon, NY, since 2002. https://spiritfirefestival.org/

July **Starwood Festival,** Pomeroy, OH, since 1981. www.starwoodfestival.com/

Aug. **CWPN's Harvest Gathering**, *Camp Cedarcrest, Orange, CT, since 2008.* www.cwpn.org/hg/

Aug. **Dragonfest**, Myers Ranch near Bailey, CO. https://dragonfest.org/

Aug. **Faerieworlds,** https://faerieworlds.com/

Aug. **Forestdance,** MA. https://forestdance.org/

Aug. **HexFest**, New Orleans, LA. www.hexfest.com

Aug. **Kaleidoscope Gathering,** since 1989. www.kaleidoscope-gathering.com/

Aug. **Mėnuo Juodaragis,** since 1995. www.mjr.lt/XXII/en/

Aug. **Sacred Harvest Festival**, Harmony Tribe, Atchingtan, Finlayson, MN, since 1997. www.harmonytribe.org/

Aug. **Templefest**, Summer Festival of the Temple of Witchcraft, since 2010. http://templefest.templeofwitchcraft.org

Sept. **Magickal Mountain Mabon**, Ardantane, NM. www.ardantane.org

Sept. **Pagan Pride Day,** held annually at many locations since 1992. https://en.wikipedia.org/wiki/Pagan_Pride

Sept. **Stones Rising**, Four Quarters Farm, Artemas, PA, since 1995. www.4qf.org/values/age-of-limits/74-event-pages/stones-rising

Oct. **Autumn Meet**, Solomon Springs, FL. www.phoenixfestivals.com/

Oct. **FallFling**, Roxanna, Auburn, AL. www.faeriefaith.net/Fall-Fling.shtml

Oct. **CascadiaFire**, WA, since 2015. www.cascadiafire.com

Oct. **FallFest**, Las Vegas, NV. www.VegasVortex.com

Oct. **Hekate's Sickle Festival,** WA, since 1989. www.sickle.atcwicca.org

Oct. **Midwest Witches'Ball**, Royalty House, Warren, MI. http://midwestwitchesball.com/

Oct. **Twilight Covening,** MA, since 1986. www.earthspirit.com/events

Nov. **Trees of Avalon Gathering**, Silver Spring, FL. https://tagmeet.org

Dec. **Hawkfest Yule**, Bonita Springs, FL. https://www.facebook.com/groups/175031977219/

Mo? **Untamed**, Parrish Ranch, Berthoud, CO. https://untamedfest.com

Pagan Events by Squirrelly Productions, Spokane, WA. http://squirrellyproductions.weebly.com/

Canadian Pagan Festivals

www.patheos.com/blogs/betweentheshadows/2015/05/all-the-canadian-pagan-festivals/

Australian Pagan Festivals

Jan. **Pagan Summer Gathering** (PSG); Church of All Worlds, since 1998. http://www.caw.org.au/

May **Mount Franklin Pagan Gathering,** Victoria, NSW, since 1981. https://mountfranklinpagans.wordpress.com/

Sept. **Australian Wiccan Conference,** since 1984. https://business.facebook.com/AustralianWiccanConference/

Pagan-owned temples, sanctuaries & festival sites (US)

Ardantane, (1996). www.ardantane.org
Atchingtan (Harmony Tribe), Finlayson, MN. www.harmonytribe.org/
All World Acres, Tampa, FL. http://healingto-day.com/all_world_acres.htm
Annwfn (CAW), Redwood Valley, CA. https://annwfn.org/
Brushwood Folklore Center, Sherman, NY. www.brushwood.com
Camp Cedarcrest (CWPN), Orange, CT. www.cwpn.org/hg/
Camp Midian, Springville, IN. http://www.campmidian.com/
The Catskills Phygianum of the Maetreum of Cybele, Palenville, NY
Ceren Ered, Cosby, TN. https://business.facebook.com/cerrenered/
Circle Sanctuary, Barneveld, WI. www.circlesanctuary.org
Dragon Hills, Carrolton, GA.
Four Quarters Interfaith Sanctuary, Artemas, PA. https://4qf.org/
Gaea Retreat Center, McLouth, KS. https://gaearetreat.org/
Goddus Mountain, Montague, MA. www.schoolofsophia.com/
The Goddess Temple of Ashland, OR
Isis Oasis, Geyserville, CA. http://isisoasissanctuary.org/
The Longhouse Spiritual Sanctuary, Redmond, WA. https://venu-sian.church/
Lothlorien Nature Sanctuary, Bedford/Needmore, IN. https://elvin-home.org/
Camp Midian, Springville, IN. www.campmidian.com/
NewGrange Hall Asatru Hof, Brownsville, CA
Oak Spirit Sanctuary, MO. www.oakspiritsanctuary.org/
Our Haven Nature Sanctuary, French Lick, IN. www.ourhaven.info
Raven's Knoll, Eganville, ON, Canada. https://ravensknoll.ca/
Roxanna, Auburn, AL. http://www.roxannaland.org/
RUNVira Temple of Mother Ukraine-Oryana, Spring Glen, NY
Sacred Land (Earth Spirit), Williamsburg, MA. www.earth-spirit.com/events/sacred-land
Seelie Court (Assembly of Sacred Wheel), Georgetown, DE. www.sa-credwheel.org
Spirit Haven Ranch (CMA), Flatonia, TX
Temple of Goddess Spirituality, Indian Springs, NV. https://www.sekhmettemple.org/
Thor's Hollow Retreat (ADF), Cross Junction, VA
Tredara (ADF), OH
Trout Lake Abbey (ADF), Trout Lake, WA. www.tlabbery.com
Wisteria Event Site, Pomeroy, OH. www.wisteria.org/
Wite Rayvn Metaphysical Church, MO. http://witerayvn.org/

f.
select bibliography

resources & references—online:

British Traditional Wicca, https://en.wikipedia.org/wiki/British_Traditional_Wicca

Canadian Pagan Festivals. www.patheos.com/blogs/betweentheshadows/2015/05/all-the-canadian-pagan-festivals/

Circle Sanctuary. "History of Circle Sanctuary" [http://www.circlesanctuary.org/aboutcircle/timeline.htm]

Linda's List of Pagan Festivals. www.faeriefaith.net/festival.list.html

List of modern Pagan temples. https://en.wikipedia.org/wiki/List_of_modern_Pagan_temples

List of NeoPagan movements, https://en.wikipedia.org/wiki/List_of_NeoPagan_movements

"The McFarland Dianics–A Chronology" www.mcfarlanddianic.org/a-chronology.php

Modern Paganism. https://en.wikipedia.org/wiki/Modern_Paganism

NeoPaganism in the United States. https://en.wikipedia.org/wiki/NeoPaganism_in_the_United_States#Organizations

Ontario Consultants on Religious Tolerance. http://www.religioustolerance.org/wic_news.htm

"Paganism," The Pluralism Project, Harvard University. https://pluralism.org/Paganism

Encyclopædia Britannica, s.v. "Neo-Paganism

further reading:

Adler, Margot, *Drawing Down the Moon: Witches, Druids, Goddess-Worshippers, and Other Pagans in America.* Penguin Books, 1979; 1987; 2006.

Barrett, David V., *A Brief Guide to Magical & Secret Religions.* Constable & Robinson/ Running Press, 2011.

Berger, Helen A., *A Community of Witches: Contemporary Neo-Paganism and Witchcraft in the United States.* University of South Carolina Press, 1999.

_____, *Witchcraft and Magic: Contemporary North America.* University of South Carolina Press, 2005.

Bonewits, P.E.I.B. & Phaedra, *Real Energy: Systems, Spirits, and Substances to Heal, Change, and Grow.* New Page Books, 2007.

Burnett, David. *Dawning of the Pagan Moon* (1991)

Clifton, Chas S., *Her Hidden Children: The Rise of Wicca & Paganism in America.* Altamira Press, 2006.

Cowan, Douglas E., *Cyberhenge: Modern Pagans on the Internet.* Routledge, 2004.

Downey, Kathryn. "Spiritual Dandelions" in *Feminist Foremothers in Women's Studies, Psychology, and Mental Health* (1995)

Ellwood, Robert S. & Partin, Harry B., *Religious and Spiritual Groups in Modern America.* Pearson College Div. 1988; 1998.

Ellwood, "Notes on a Neopagan Religious Group in America," *History of Religions*, Vol. 11, No. 1 (1971)

Fitch, Ed. A Grimoire of Shadows (1996), especially "Preface," excepts by Sylvana SilverWitch in "Ed Fitch: Revealing the Craft," *Widdershins,* vol. 1, no. 2 (1995)

Gruagach, Ben. *The Wiccan Mystic: Exploring a Magickal Spiritual Path* (2007)

Guiley, Rosemary, *Encyclopedia of Witches & Witchcraft.* Facts on File, 1989; 1999; 2008.

Harvey, Graham, *Contemporary Paganism: Listening People, Speaking Earth.* NY Univ. Press, 1997.

_____, & Hardman, Charlotte, eds. *Paganism Today.* Thorsons Press, 1995.

Hawkins, Craig, *Goddess Worship, Witchcraft and Neo-Paganism.* Zondervan Publishing, 1998.

Hopman, Ellen Evert, *Being a Pagan: Druids, Wiccans, and Witches Today.* Inner Traditions/Destiny Books, 2001.

_____ & Bond, Lawrence, *People of the Earth: The New Pagans Speak Out,* Inner Traditions/Destiny Books, 1996.

Howard, Mike. "Gerald Gardner: The Man, the Myth & the Magick"

Hutton, Ronald. "The Roots of Modern Paganism," in Harvey, Graham, *Paganism Today* (1996)

_____, *Triumph of the Moon: A History of Modern Pagan Witchcraft.* Oxford University Press, 2000.

Kelly, Aidan A., *A Tapestry of Witches: A History of the Craft in America, Vol. I, to the Mid-1970s.* CreateSpace Independent Publishing Platform, 2014.

_____, *Hippie Commie Beatnik Witches: A History of the Craft in California,* 1967-77 (1993)

_____, *History of Neopagan and Magickal Groups in the USA and Canada*

Lamond, Frederic. *Fifty Years of Wicca* (2005)

Lewis, James R., ed. *Magical Religion & Modern Witchcraft*. State University of New York, 1996.

Lipp, Deborah, & Bonewits, Isaac. *The Study of Witchcraft: A Guidebook to Advanced Wicca* (2007)

Melton, J. Gordon, *Encyclopedia of American Religions*. Gale / Cengage Learning, 1979; 1991; 2003.

_____ & Poggi, I, Magic, *Witchcraft, and Paganism in America*, 1992.

_____ & Partridge, Christopher, *eds. New Religions: A Guide: New Religious Movements, Sects and Alternative Spiritualities*. Oxford University Press, 2004.

Miller, Timothy, ed., *America's Alternative Religions*. State University of New York Press, 1995

Muntean, F.D. "Wicca After Starhawk" (1995)

Myers, Brendan, *The Earth, the Gods and the Soul–A History of Pagan Philosophy from the Iron Age to the 21st Century*. Moon Books, 2013

Orion, Loretta, *Never Again the Burning Times: Paganism Revived*. Waveland Press, 1995.

Pearson, Jo. "Demarcating the Field: Paganism, Wicca, & Witchcraft" in DISKUS, vol. 6 (2000)

Pike, Sarah M, *New Age and NeoPagan Religions in America*. Columbia University Press, 2004; 2006.

Rabinovitch, Shelly & Lewis, James, *Encyclopedia of Modern Witchcraft & Neo-Paganism*. Citadel, 2002.

Starhawk. *The Spiral Dance: A Rebirth of the Ancient Religion of the Goddess* (1979, 1999, 2009)

Townsend, Mark, *Jesus Through Pagan Eyes*. Llewellyn, 2012.

Vale, V. & Sulak, John, *Modern Pagans: An Investigation of Contemporary Pagan Practices*. ReSearch Books, 2001.

Waldron, David. *The Sign of the Witch: Modernity and the Pagan Revival* (2008)

_____, & Sharn. "Jung and the Neo-Pagan Movement," *Quadrant*, vol. 34, No. 2 (Summer 2004)

Wicke, Christine, *Not in Kansas Anymore: A Curious Tale of How Magic is Transforming America*. HarperSanFrancisco, 2005.

Wilson, Joseph Bearwalker, *So You Wanna Be A Shaman, Eh?* (2011)

Wynn, Anita L., *Odyssey: Wisdom's Children*. PublishAmerica, 2006.

Zell, Oberon, *Grimoire for the Apprentice Wizard,* with the Grey Council. New Page Books (2004)

_____, *Companion for the Apprentice Wizard*, with the Faculty of the Grey School of Wizardry (New Page Books, 2006)

www.ingramcontent.com/pod-product-compliance
Lightning Source LLC
Chambersburg PA
CBHW030827090426
42737CB00009B/905